MW00458859

"Sadly, the kinds of w navigate our relationship with the most important, most precious person in our lives can be careless, hurtful, and alienating. In this book, Rob Flood applies biblical insight to unhealthy patterns of communication, offering genuine hope to couples who long for a marriage in which words are used to affirm, connect, and bless."

Nancy Guthrie, Author; Bible teacher

"Your words bring life or death to your most important relationships. Healthy communication in marriage is like blood to the body—it is the life giver to every marriage. Rob's authenticity and biblical approach to communication in marriage and life will be a fresh, life-giving transfusion for all your relationships."

Dennis Rainey, Cofounder, FamilyLife

"In a Twitter world, most of us have become way too casual about the words we speak every day. Words have so much power! They can build up a marriage or tear it down. This book will be a turning point for a lot of marriages. It gives us the help we need to know how to use our words wisely and carefully."

Bob Lepine, Cohost, *FamilyLife Today*

"*With These Words* serves as a marriage toolbox, providing the tools people need to strengthen a healthy marriage and rekindle hope and inject fresh faith for couples in conflict. This is the marriage book pastors have been looking for to use with their couples' ministry or married small group. *With These Words* is scripturally rich, theologically grounded, and filled with practical application to make this book a must read for every married couple."

Marty Machowski, Family pastor; author of *The Ology*, *Parenting First Aid*, *Long Story Short*, and other gospel rich resources for church and home

"Whether your marriage is happy or hurting, every couple needs help communicating. Rob Flood is a skilled counselor with years of pastoral experience in strengthening marriages. The unique value of this book is its focus on practical application, and the insistence that God's truth must function in everyday marital communication. I can't wait to get *With These Words* into the hands of married couples in our church and beyond."

Jared Mellinger, Author of *Think Again* and *A Bright Tomorrow*

"My recommendation begins with the author. I know Rob Flood. He pastors with me in our church. He has helped me be a better husband and father and communicator. I often pass by his office and see married couples sitting with him—couples who can't resolve their problems because they don't even know how to talk about them. I'm glad they're in his office. Rob helps people change. I've seen it with my own eyes. This book is your opportunity to see it in your own life."

Andy Farmer, Pastor; author of *Real Peace* and *Trapped*; council member, the Biblical Counseling Coalition

"Communication is challenging. Some, however, limit their understanding of communication—their view is too small. *With These Words* reminds us that communication is a much deeper issue than we realize. Since our words are an outflow of the heart, every aspect of our heart impacts our communication. That is why prayer is so important. It is why timing is so important. It is why your closeness with Jesus is so important. You will find help for both your heart and for your tongue in this book."

Rob Green, Pastor of Counseling and Seminary Ministries at Faith Church, Lafayette, Indiana; author of *Tying the Knot* and coauthor of *Tying their Shoes*

With These Words

With These Words

Five Communication Tools
for Marriage and Life

Rob Flood

New
Growth
Press
WWW.NEWGROWTHPRESS.COM

New Growth Press, Greensboro, NC 27404
www.newgrowthpress.com

With These Words is based on the article "5 Communication Tools That
Saved My Marriage" © Copyright 2005 by FamilyLife, published at
http://www.familylife.com/articles/topics/marriage/staying-married/
communication/5-communication-tools-that-saved-my-marriage. Used by
permission of FamilyLife.

Cover Design: Faceout Books, faceoutstudios.com
Interior Typesetting and eBook: LParnell Book Services

ISBN: 978-1-64507-042-9 (Print)
ISBN: 978-1-64507-043-6 (eBook)

Library of Congress Cataloging-in-Publication Data
Names: Flood, Rob, 1971– author.
Title: With these words : five communication tools for marriage and life /
    by Rob Flood.
Description: Greensboro, NC : New Growth Press, [2020] | Includes biblio-
    graphical references. | Summary: "All couples need clear communication,
    especially in the face of obstacles. Rob Flood teaches practical, biblical
    wisdom for couples interested in growing in their marriages together toward
    Christ. Learn to better understand your partner and remain as God made
    you, all while honoring Christ with your words"— Provided by publisher.
Identifiers: LCCN 2019034690 (print) | LCCN 2019034691 (ebook) | ISBN
    9781645070429 (trade paperback) | ISBN 9781645070436 (ebook)
Subjects: LCSH: Marriage—Religious aspects—Christianity. | Communica-
    tion in marriage. | Communication—Religious aspects—Christianity.
Classification: LCC BV835 .F549 2020 (print) | LCC BV835 (ebook) |
    DDC 248.8/44—dc23
LC record available at https://lccn.loc.gov/2019034690
LC ebook record available at https://lccn.loc.gov/2019034691

Printed in the United States of America
27 26 25 24 23 22 21 20   1 2 3 4 5

Contents

Acknowledgements

BOOKS ARE FUNNY things. A person's name appears on the front (in this case, it's mine). Yet, the book is a product of community that occurs over a lifetime. As those in my church read this book, they likely see my fingerprints all over it. As I read this book, I see the fingerprints of men and women who have built into my life for decades. Their voices ring in my mind. Their sacrifices of time, talent, and treasure echo in my heart. They are the ones I acknowledge here.

First and foremost, I am grateful to God for providing me a wife like Gina. Her intelligence, humility, boldness, studiousness, curiosity, insightfulness, and silliness have made the journey of marital discipleship a joy and a privilege. She has borne the impact of my communication mistakes, my selfishness, and my immaturity as we've grown and matured together. If I could do it all over again, I'd still pick you, Gina. I'd just do it more quickly.

After Gina, my children have heard more of my words than anyone else. They, too, have needed to forebear as I've learned the similarities and differences between marital and parental communication. Nate, Sam, Hannah, James, Lizzy, and Jenny, thank you for supporting the process of this book, for sacrificing time with me, and for being bold to mold and shape me as a dad.

My parents, Larry and Rita Flood, modeled a marriage of mutual sacrifice and respect. Through countless and seemingly immeasurable trials, they provided a high view of marriage that formed my own view of marriage. Though my father is now with the Lord, his voice continues to ring forth next to my mom's calling me to higher roads.

Ralph and Pat Ricci, the dear parents I married into, modeled faithfulness for the woman who has been faithful to me. They befriended my parents, continue to love and serve my mother, and remain steadfast as they exemplify what marriage-for-the-long-haul can look like.

Barbara Juliani and the editing team at New Growth Press have had endless patience with me as we, together, crafted the volume you're about to read. Thank you, New Growth Press, for helping me craft and publish a message that can serve marriages and families.

My invaluable experience at FamilyLife grew me as a writer and a thinker, both theologically and technically. For that, I have Bob Lepine and David Boehi to thank. David was the ever-gracious yet never-relenting editor who knew when I could provide better and would never settle for less than my best. Bob was the theological voice who could condense an hour's worth of discipleship into fifteen minutes. I'm indebted to both men for the trust and dedication they showed me during my time there.

Nearly twenty men and women sat with my manuscript at its earliest stage—before edits, rewrites, and submission to the publisher. These reviewers included younger and older, men and women, pastors and laity. They sacrificed time and invested wisdom that can be traced throughout the book.

Thank you for your willingness to be the first readers that read this book and the first voices that spoke into it.

Many pastors have made meaningful investments into me as a man, a husband, a father, and a pastor. The first one was John Mitchell. Our time together, John, seems like ages ago (because it was ages ago). However, your humility and unwavering love for the church, even when it was seemingly unlovable, continues to be a source of wisdom for me in my ministry.

I have been indelibly marked by the teaching ministries of two men I've met but I'm certain have no recollection of meeting me. Alistair Begg from Parkside Church near Cleveland and Joe Focht from Calvary Chapel of Philadelphia are two men who will only know their impact when they receive their crowns in glory. Through the beauty of Christian radio, I sat under them both during my most formative theological years.

Lastly, there is the church where I now serve: Covenant Fellowship Church in Glen Mills, Pennsylvania. Jared Mellinger, our senior pastor, has created an environment where the unique gifts of the team can thrive. Marty Machowski has been a constant support, from assisting with my book proposal to continued aid throughout the writing process. Along with those men, the pastors and wives the Lord has positioned at Covenant Fellowship, past and present, are gifts from God as friends and as co-laborers. Ministry is a joy, fellowship a privilege, and friendship a safe place because of your grace and godliness. I must include the dearest members of Christ's church, the saints of Covenant Fellowship Church. Your friendships with our family are hallmarks of Christian love and faithfulness.

May God in his grace grant these folks a double portion of the grace they've extended to me, for his glory and the good of his church.

Introduction

Our Story

To understand our story,* we have to go back to the beginning. It was in most respects a typical Italian-American engagement. (I know "Flood" doesn't sound very Italian. My father was Irish, my mother was Italian, but our family culture was Italian indeed.) Our families were deeply involved. In fact, the night I proposed, I planned a surprise party with both sides of the family awaiting the arrival of the newly engaged couple. (That party would have been very awkward had her answer been "no"!) The one, ill-advised characteristic of our engagement was its length; we were engaged for twenty months… twenty long months.

But even at that, it was a sweet time of anticipation. As we approached the wedding date, some tensions began to brew, but it was easy to write them off as pre-wedding jitters combined with the stress of planning a once-in-a-lifetime celebration with 175 of our closest family and friends. We didn't often

---

* Except for myself and my wife, all couples mentioned in this book are fictional and there is no intention to reflect anyone specific, either in name or situation.

talk about the tensions; we just overlooked them (or so we thought) and moved on blissfully to our wedding day.

Even in light of the story that follows, the wedding day is still a treasured memory of God's kindness and grace to us. We went from our happiest *day* on earth to the "happiest *place* on earth" as we honeymooned in Disney World. If you are able to do it in the "all-inclusive honeymoon-type" way we did it, I highly recommend it.

From the start, the treatment we received in Disney should have made it easy to have a delightful and peace-filled honeymoon. However, intimacy seemed relationally awkward. We had no trouble enjoying the venue and especially the food, but we were not connecting well with each other in intimacy. These were not the normal "we just need more practice" challenges. Trust seemed shaky. Walls were up. Something was genuinely amiss.

Then it happened...*day five*. It was technically day six of the marriage, but it was day five at the "happiest place on earth." In our hotel room, that beautiful, posh, Yacht Club room, we had the biggest fight of our marriage. I don't mean the biggest fight of our six-day-old marriage. I mean the biggest fight of our now two-decade-plus marriage. Things were said that you just don't come back from. We threw word grenades without consideration for any of the lasting damage that would come from the shrapnel of our bad intentions. We were Christians, but you never would have detected that had you been a fly on those beautiful, posh, Yacht Club walls.

Somewhere during that conflict, we both realized what a massive mistake we had made. Not the kind of humble recognition that acknowledges our words were mistakes. No, we both became convinced that our marriage was a mistake. Gina left the room and I had no idea where she went. Did I go after her? Did I worry and pray for her? No, I went to sleep. That's right. In the middle of that cataclysmic Thursday afternoon, I went to sleep.

After a couple of hours, it was time to go eat another unbelievable meal, so we put on our nicest clothes and sat across a table from one another. Our wait staff, knowing we were on our honeymoon (because people at Disney know *everything*), greeted us like the happy couple we were supposed to be. We managed to get through the remainder of the trip and make it back to our home. I wish I could end the story there and tell you that's as bad as it got. There is more.

The next nine months devolved past arguing into an icy, silent war. We didn't talk much, but everything we did say was an offense to the other. I would ask, "What's for dinner?" She would hear, "I can't believe you haven't prepared dinner again tonight!" She would say, "What time are you coming home?" I would hear, "You better get here and help me because you're never here."

We could not express anything without mistrusting and misconstruing what the other was saying. We did not build each other up. We tore each other down and caused devastating, emotional pain that settled into deep, relational scars. Quite honestly, we had inflicted so much pain on each other that we could not see any hope for ever communicating well. Our despair was overwhelming. We were both convinced that we were condemned to a loveless marriage since we had obviously married the wrong person.

Neither of us had any history of conflict like this. In fact, individually, we were both quite good at dealing with difficult situations and difficult people. We each were skilled at expressing both thoughts and feelings in words—just not with one another.

During this season of our marriage, we were meaningfully involved with our local church and in caring for others. Our church family would innocently ask, "How are the happy new-lyweds?" Neither of us could admit how poorly we were doing and how much we regretted where our lives were so we'd smile and say, "Great!" That's the answer they were looking for so no one pressed further. (For the record, I no longer give newly-weds the benefit of the doubt. I just assume they feel in over their heads, and I'm generally right.)

After five months of marriage counseling (where we were assigned many tasks but never asked to open a Bible), I finally had enough. In a moment of spiteful exasperation, I relented on a major point of conflict. Notice I did not say "I repented." There was nothing of God or grace perceptible in what I did—just exasperation, spite, and self. (When I think of the evil words that spewed forth out of my mouth, I am still brought to tears two decades later.) But my motivation didn't matter to Gina—she didn't like me anyway. I relented, and that was enough. It wasn't reconciliation by any means. But it was then that God moved.

Inexplicably, following that wicked exchange of self-ishness, God had mercy on us. The small crack created by my sinful relenting was the opening God used to pour his grace into our war-torn marriage. We spent the next several months discovering the mercy and grace of God through pas-toral help, marital conversations, prayer and confession, and the FamilyLife Weekend to Remember. It was like discover-ing a military hospital in a war zone: so much self-inflicted destruction, so much devastation, so many gaping wounds to stitch up. We learned it is harder to face reality and take responsibility than it is to assign it. But God's grace is greater than our sin.

In the process of this self-revelation and God-discovery, we both asked for and received forgiveness from each other and set our eyes on building a different future. We applied the truths of the gospel. We never wanted to go back to that dark and destructive place, so we learned how to communicate: how to hear and not just assume, how to speak and not just accuse, how to love by listening, and how to be on the same team—even in disagreement. But more importantly, we learned that the Word of God has much to say for couples who want to grow in their communication.

Let me be clear: God saved our marriage; we did not. God grew our communication; the tools did not. We are very much still in process. We do not have it all figured out. That is not just some self-deprecating statement authors have to make to sound humble. We still have to return to the basics over and over again. We still have struggles with communication and find ourselves still stinging every now and then from past hurts. The difference is this: There is grace now. There is charity toward one another. There is the benefit of the doubt. There are follow-up questions before there are conclusions. There is not perfection, but there is health. This is all because of God's grace working through our devotion to the Lordship of Christ and the application of basic communication tools.

This book exists to equip as many people as possible with some helpful tools for communication. These tools can help each husband and wife grow more competent and effective in their use of the powerful gift of communication—not for their own glory, but for the glory of God.

The Road Map of the Book

We are going to explore the road that Gina and I discovered. In *Section 1: Truth for Communication*, we will find the rule book, the user's manual for communication. This section does not contain everything the Bible says about the topic, but it contains some key passages that we discovered were full of God's wisdom. We need that kind of biblical foundation before we proceed to *Section 2: Tools for Communication*. This is the practical application of the user's manual. Some application comes directly from the Scriptures and some comes from personal experience. Then in *Section 3: Working It Out*, we will learn how to move forward safely, successfully, and soundly in the will of God.

This book is written to be helpful. I'm hopeful each section will improve your communication. Yet, for our communication to change, we must change. We must be willing to see our weaknesses, to see what is beyond our reach, and to embrace true power to change. That power comes to us from God through his Son. Without his power at work in our lives, these tools will be like a power drill that remains unplugged. Without his power, we will walk around our marital communication as we might a living room with the lights off. We'll stumble and fall without much success.

Jesus tells us that we are incapable of doing anything of value, of bearing any real fruit, apart from him (John 15). Allow the tools and tips and helps found in the pages that follow to reveal your need for God's power, for a surrendered life, for a life lived for his purposes and his glory. Then, with your weaknesses freshly revealed, turn to the one who makes his power perfect in them (2 Corinthians 12). When your life is connected to his, when you are living under his direction, you will see much fruit indeed.

Before proceeding, it is necessary to make one qualifying statement here. The principles and truths contained in this book are useful for most couples. However, they are not intended to be a substitute for pastoral care, for the fellowship of the saints, nor for civil authorities when that is appropriate. While the principles in this book are good and helpful, if you are in an abusive situation, you ought not to stay in that situation attempting to work on communication. Instead, notify the authorities, a pastor, or a good friend as the situation demands. By God's grace, there will come a time, after your safety is secured and God's grace moves on your spouse that this book will be useful in your marriage, but your safety must come first.

Now, as we get started, let me ask you to pray. Pray that God would reveal your weaknesses and sins in communication rather than you focusing on the faults of your spouse. Pray that God would bring more than clarity, but also conviction, insight, and hope. Also, consider sharing with a friend or pastor that you are reading a book on honoring God with your words, and ask them to pray for your marriage and check in with you on how it's going.

In fact, let me be the first to pray with you now.

Heavenly Father, this brother or sister reading this book has a context in which they're reading. Perhaps their marriage is struggling and they're looking for hope. Perhaps their marriage is thriving and they're being proactive. I do not know their situation, but you know it fully. You know our thoughts, and before a word is on our tongues you know it. Father, draw near to them at this time, fulfilling your promises: to be a present help in their time of trouble (Psalm 46:1), to be near to the brokenhearted (Psalm 34:18), and to shine a light on the hope and future you have for them and their marriage (Jeremiah 29:11). Spirit, fill them with understanding and provide help as you walk alongside them in their reading. Apply what is best, and help them to discard the rest. We pray in Jesus's holy and precious name, Amen.

Section 1:

Truth for Communication

WHETHER YOU HAVE a wonderful marriage or are experiencing troubles, we all can agree that healthy communication is a fundamental part of a strong relationship between a husband and wife. So we start this journey where all journeys must start: knowing where we're going. We start with knowledge.

To be a Christian is to believe the Bible is inspired by God and given to us for life and godliness (2 Timothy 3). It is to believe that the Bible has authority in our lives (Matthew 4:4), that we are changed by *it* and not the other way around (Hebrews 4:12–13). This is why I invite you to start this journey by understanding what the Bible says about words, their purpose, and effect.

The words that pass our lips don't start on our tongues. No, their origin goes a bit deeper into the body—into the heart (Matthew 12:34). Our words all start in our soul. Our mouths are morally neutral; all they do is *express* the morality or immorality, the faith or unbelief, the love of others or self, that is contained in our hearts.

Words contain the immense power to carry such messages as the gospel of Jesus Christ and the hope of eternity to come. When we are careless with our words, we cheapen the currency of communication and weaken the bonds that hold relationships together. So let's begin the journey of learning about words and discover together what God intends for his children as they use them.

Discussion/Reflection Questions

Preparing for Section One

1. What was communication like in your childhood home? In what ways do you see those patterns of communication in your life today?

2. If you could rate your marital communication on a scale from 1 to 10, how would you rate it? Why?

3. What one or two main things do you believe need to occur for the communication in your marriage to improve?

Chapter 1

Use Only as Directed

*When God spoke, everything listened. Everything responded
to God because he spoke – everything except humans.*[1]
- Gary Edward Schnittjer

*Let no corrupting talk come out of your mouths,
but only such as is good for building up, as fits the occasion,
that it may give grace to those who hear.*
- Ephesians 4:29

Yeah, Let's Talk…Oh Wait, Not about That

Tom and Marcy Butler are relatively new members at First
Community Church after coming from another local church in
the area. Each of them has experienced a pretty rough divorce
and spent a number of years raising their children alone. After
working through the initial shock and tragedy of the ending
to their first marriages, they separately sought to grow as indi-
viduals and as disciples. When they met, they committed to
starting their relationship as friends. They certainly were not
going to rush things.

Once they became a couple, they sought help from their
pastors and attended conferences to equip themselves for the
potential of marriage. As they applied themselves, they seemed
to excel at communication. More mature couples even began

asking for their help in their own marital challenges. Tom and Marcy feel like they've been through the fire and desire to be a blessing to others at First Community.

Their home is marked with carefulness and tenderness. Arguments are rare, as they seem to be able to walk through the most challenging topics with love and grace. By all counts, they are a healthy married couple honoring God as they honor one another.

However, there is a glitch not known to those around them. Their sexual intimacy is a challenging element in their marriage. Neither Marcy nor Tom is happy about it, but they don't know how to talk about it. Marcy's first husband had an affair so Marcy is understandably sensitive to this topic. Tom's first marriage ended after years of volatile conflicts with his first wife.

When they tried in the past, it didn't go well. The subject seems to short-circuit their carefulness in speech. Marcy gets emotional and uses words that are harsh and defensive. Tom withdraws, ultimately using quiet, but angry words to make it clear that he's not the problem. In the one area where their communication is in greatest need of carefulness, they can't seem to achieve it.

The mixture of Marcy's sensitivity to the topic and Tom's desire to avoid arguments at all cost has caused their sex life to go unaddressed. They don't want the conflict that ensues, so they avoid it. The problems are still there because they can't seem to use the right words in the right way at the most crucial time.

The Problem Illustrated

The way the Butlers communicate reminds me of Christmas, 2004. A family friend gave our sons a tool kit complete with a small hammer, a tape measure, and two precision screwdrivers.

You know, the tiny screwdrivers used for glasses. My five-year-old went right to work, hammering nails through boards straight into our deck.

Inspired by his older brother, my three-year-old attempted the same. His nail, however, was strangely larger than the one his older brother was using. Upon further examination, it became clear that he pulled the flat-head precision screwdriver from his kit and used it as a nail. The logic is impeccable: the head is larger and it was easier to hold. Forever damaged, the purpose of the screwdriver's brief existence was to become memorialized in this illustration. Even though his intentions were wonderful, he grossly misused the tool and significantly damaged it.

The Communication Connection

Among the other challenges the Butlers may be facing, they share something in common with my son. In the most sensitive times, they are using words differently from their intended design. They are harsh and uncaring when talking about their intimacy. They use their words to defend or attack. Their solution to this problem is to avoid words altogether when it comes to intimacy, which fixes one problem while creating others. And just like the screwdriver, significant damage can be done to their marriage either way, even if it's unintentional.

In light of how important words are, let's investigate together how to use words in our marriages. Let's educate ourselves and fill our minds with truth that can transform our hearts, our communication, and our marriages.

Husbands and wives don't need to settle for the challenges facing the Butlers. We don't have to settle for any of our weaknesses and sins in communication. With the power of God and the help of the Spirit under the guidance and authority of the Scriptures, couples claiming to follow Christ can do better than this. As a means of communication, words are designed to leave an aroma of Christ, to dispense grace, to express love, and to give life. When we fail to direct the purpose of our words this way, we are not living as disciples. You may get what you want in the moment if you're sarcastic or mean or hurtful, but in the long run, those careless words will do more than damage your marriage. One day you will be called to give an account for every one of them (Matthew 12:36).

The Ultimate Purpose of Communication

At the end of the day, after we peel back all of the complicated layers, the ultimate purpose of all communication is to glorify God and reflect his image with our words. I know that might seem too lofty to be helpful. However, let's break it down, and we'll see just how useful it is.

As Christians, all we say and do is supposed to have the purpose of bringing glory to God. Consider the following familiar passages from Paul's letters:

> Therefore be imitators of God, as beloved children. And walk in love, as Christ loved us and gave himself up for us, a fragrant offering and sacrifice to God. (Ephesians 5:1–2)

> And whatever you do, in word or deed, do everything in the name of the Lord Jesus, giving thanks to God the Father through him. (Colossians 3:17)

> I appeal to you therefore, brothers, by the mercies of God, to present your bodies as a living sacrifice, holy and acceptable to God, which is your spiritual worship. (Romans 12:1)

14

When God redeems us, he makes a wholesale claim on our lives (Isaiah 43:1). Gloriously, we are free from the penalty of our sin and ransomed from death to life (1 Peter 1:18–19). That salvation is the beginning of a relationship with Jesus where he is in charge. We were once slaves to sin; we are now slaves to righteousness (Romans 6:18). We've been liberated *from* a master who only had destruction planned for us. We've been delivered *to* a master who only has good planned for us. We no longer have a devious dictator, but a benevolent Lord (Romans 6:22). These redemptive truths mean that each element of our lives is to be lived for Christ, including our words.

In capturing the impact our redemption is to have in our lives, the apostle Peter says this:

> Whoever speaks, as one who speaks oracles of God; whoever serves, as one who serves by the strength that God supplies—in order that in everything God may be glorified through Jesus Christ. To him belong glory and dominion forever and ever. Amen. (1 Peter 4:11)

God's claim on us is all-encompassing. In all things, God is supposed to be glorified in the lives of those who call upon his name for salvation. This is the result of the indwelling of the Spirit in our lives. He moves and directs our hearts, which overflow with his purposes and not ours. This is the only way that fallen and finite creatures like us could speak as those who are speaking the utterances of God.

When we see this truth, moved by the Spirit, our hearts want to walk in the goodness of it. Knowing that Christ laid everything down for us, we in turn want to lay everything down in order to walk with him and keep in step with his Spirit

(Galatians 5:25). To do this, there are four key principles that function as user instructions for our communication. These, more than any personal objectives, need to shape our words. The first flows right out of 1 Peter 4:11.

Principle 1: We should speak so people encounter God.

As ambassadors for Christ, we represent him and his purposes everywhere we go. Our words are not our own, and when we speak it ought not represent *our* will, but *his* will. When your husband fails to show gratitude for your hard work, you remain an ambassador for Christ. The words you speak in response to that injustice will reflect either your will or God's will. When your wife says something you find to be careless and hurtful, you are still an ambassador for Christ, and your words are still supposed to sound like God himself might say them.

When we speak, people should encounter God, not us. If they are blessed by what you say, it is because God provides the blessing. If they are offended by what you say, it ought to be because they are offended at what God had to say and not offended because of you.

The Scriptures are full of examples of men and women receiving injustice, who had a legitimate case for responding harshly. Yet many of them manifested the reality and wisdom of 1 Peter 4:11.

Paul Attacked in Ephesus (Acts 19): An amazing work of the Spirit was happening through Paul. It turned Ephesus on its head and left many residents and merchants unhappy with him. Were they incensed at Paul's personality or tone or were they offended by the truth that he spoke? Paul was speaking as one who speaks oracles of God, and those truths offended them. They didn't primarily encounter Paul; they encountered God.

Nathan before David (2 Samuel 12): Following David's plot to cover his adultery with Bathsheba by murdering Uriah, Nathan the prophet was led by God to address David. Who was truly confronting David in the king's chamber? Was it Nathan the prophet or the Lord? David accepted Nathan's words as God's words, and he repented. David didn't primarily encounter Nathan; he encountered God.

Christ and the Pharisees (John 8): From the moment of his birth through the moment of his ascension, factions formed around their common hatred of Jesus. But why? Was he brash and arrogant? Did he lack compassion or wisdom? No, he was gentle and quiet in spirit, kind and compassionate. Jesus's words were God's words. And those who were opposed to God were incensed, but not because of anything Jesus did. In fact, at his trial they found no fault with him, no laws that he had broken. When they encountered Jesus, they encountered God...and they did not like it.

You may never face rioting mobs, or sinful kings, or homicidal Pharisees. You will, however, face friends, pastors, a spouse, or your children. The Lord will direct you to speak to them. The question is whose desires will you speak?

The pattern that plagued my marriage in those first couple of years was a pattern of speech that was nothing like the oracles of God. I wanted peace and comfort and a big fence built around my preferences. God wanted me to lay down my life for my wife and wash her in the water of the Word (Ephesians 5:25–26). Instead, I unleashed a firehose of my own words, robbing her of the nurturing care God calls me to express as a husband (Ephesians 5:29).

As you read, perhaps you are remembering some recent marital conversations. Perhaps your attention has been on how your spouse was not speaking the very oracles of God. Hopefully, you're also aware of how you struggle in the same area.

Remember, in the Christian life, conviction is a welcomed friend. Because God is always for us, we can be sure that conviction of sin is intended for our good (1 John 1:9). Don't push it away; invite it closer. We are called to speak in this way by the God who loves us. As his children, he empowers us to use words as he has directed since the beginning.

Principle 2: We should build up with our words and not tear down.

Principles two, three, and four capture the direction God provides in just one amazing verse: Ephesians 4:29. Paul's entire paragraph (verses 25–32) is rich with instruction that, if followed, will inevitably lead to marital blessing. The verse placed in the center of that paragraph is worthy of closer study. "Let no corrupting talk come out of your mouths, but only such as is good for building up, as fits the occasion, that it may give grace to those who hear" (Ephesians 4:29).

In the first phrase of that verse, you may wonder what Paul means when he says "corrupting." The Bible often does what Paul does here. A thought starts with stating the negative, then expounds upon it by stating the opposite, positive truth. We learn just what he means by "corrupting" when we see the kind of speech he wants us to use: not "corrupting" talk, but only "building up" talk. If we are commanded to use words that build up, then corrupting talk must be the opposite and include any words that tear down. Now we're getting someplace.

Words were designed to give life. We see this from the first moment of creation, when God spoke, and the universe came to be (Genesis 1). We are made in the image of Christ and, therefore, are designed to give life with our words. And yet, either our fallen ignorance or our willful rebellion causes us to use words to "tear down."

Have you ever said words you knew were awful the moment they left your mouth? Have you ever wanted to take back something you said the moment after it was said? What is actually happening in that experience? You hear words that land like nuclear bombs on someone you love and care for, and you know they will have radioactive impact for days, weeks, or months to come. Or maybe it is the accumulation of small, bitter words that wear away at a marriage like a moth eating fabric. You know you can never "unsay" them. They will remain in the annuls of communication history forever. You and your spouse may recover, but it won't be because of those words; it will be in spite of those words.

We can recover from words that tear down. But how much better would it be to avoid the damage in the first place? What would a marriage be like if each spouse purposed to use words that are good for building up? Even if just one spouse committed to speech that builds up, an entire marriage and an entire trajectory of the legacy of a home could be altered.

Principle 3: We should speak in a way that fits the occasion.

Ephesians 4:29 continues with four small but potent words: "as fits the occasion." Every moment has a need. Some moments have a need for silence and others have a need for many words. As speakers, we are responsible to identify the need of the moment.

You don't want a doctor to administer medication or perform a procedure without first assessing your condition. Until this happens, any action on his or her part is likely to do more harm than good. Rather, you'd expect any good doctor to take his or her time, be careful, and know that the prescribed medicine will fit the occasion of how you're feeling.

In the same way, we must be careful to assess a situation before unloading our words. If we fail to do so, even our good intentions can't prevent our careless words from doing damage. But if we are careful to understand the occasion properly, God can use our words for good.

Though every moment has a particular need, there are pockets of time that routinely call for discernment. One of those times is the last few moments before parting ways for the day. They leave a lingering flavor on the lips and, if encountered poorly, a lasting sourness to the belly. Usually the need of that moment is to protect and promote grace. We are wise to guard those times.

Then there are the first few moments when you come back together at the end of the day. Each of you has lived at least eight hours apart. During that time a lot of life has happened. In a very real sense, your spouse has changed since you last saw him or her and you don't actually have any idea what the need of that moment is. So those first few moments of reuniting are for learning and connecting. They must be approached carefully if your words are going to build up.

The last pocket of time I want to address is any time intimacy is being discussed. This is true whether we are talking about words used during sexual intimacy or in the moments leading up to and coming out of sexual intimacy. Even if you're at your dining room table talking about it, your words must be carefully chosen. Because of the unique vulnerability of sexual intimacy, your conversations about it delve more deeply into the heart and have a much longer shelf life.

Our calling before God is to speak in such a way as fits that occasion. But what if we don't know the need of the moment? What if we can't tell what would be fitting to that occasion? This is where we typically underuse an important communication tool: silence. James instructed us to be "quick to hear, slow to speak" (James 1:19). Is it possible the delay in speech is designed for us to ponder what words will be most helpful?

If words are this significant, then they should be carefully chosen, particularly in sensitive moments. As followers of Jesus and as spouses called to build a godly marriage, our words must fit the occasion.

Principle 4: We should give grace to others through our words.

If our words are going to build up, they will do more than encourage; they will help others grow more like Jesus. Ephesians 4:29 concludes with the following stipulation for our speech: "that it may give grace to those who hear."

Grace comes in many flavors and colors. Sometimes grace is sweet and complimentary. You go to a dance recital for your niece and she asks if you liked it. Your response focuses upon your joy in seeing her enjoy herself rather than your critique of the choreography or song selection, or the fact that you don't care much for dance at all. By focusing on the truth of your joy in seeing her perform, you've extended grace in a sweet and complimentary way.

At other times, grace is challenging. Perhaps you have to bring a hard word to a friend who is on the verge of making an awful decision. You know your words will sting as they go in (Proverbs 27:6), but you truly believe they will result in grace when applied. This flavor of grace is not sweet on the front end but, when spoken for the benefit of the hearer, can result in sweet fruit on the other side.

We should never assume that the flavor of grace the Lord led us to use last time is the same flavor of grace we're supposed to use this time. But there is one theme that should mark all flavors of grace: looking out for the welfare of others (Philippians 2:4).

21

Again, Jesus models this for us perfectly. Sometimes his words are sweet and encouraging. "Come to me, all who labor and are heavy laden, and I will give you rest" (Matthew 11:28). Sometimes his words go in like swallowing a giant square pill. "If anyone would come after me, let him deny himself and take up his cross and follow me" (Mark 8:34). And most potently, "Get behind me, Satan! You are a hindrance to me. For you are not setting your mind on the things of God, but on the things of man" (Matthew 16:23). But in all cases, his words reveal that he is looking out for the welfare of others.

We should do the same. We should speak in a way that gives grace. This reveals a common Achilles heel in many marriages: selfishness. You see, too often, our words are used in self-serving ways when the plain command from Scripture is to use our words for serving others. The following verse from Galatians clarifies this: "I have been crucified with Christ. It is no longer I who live, but Christ who lives in me. And the life I now live in the flesh I live by faith in the Son of God, who loved me and gave himself for me" (2:20).

We are to live the calling of laying down our lives for others. This is why the New Testament is filled with an assortment of "one another" passages: serve one another (Galatians 5:13), exhort one another (Hebrews 3:13), encourage one another (1 Thessalonians 5:11), etc. Philippians 2 calls us to consider others as more important than ourselves (see verse 3). Is there any more important "other" than the one with whom you've been made one flesh?

For example, there is no room in Christianity, let alone in marriage, for venting. Venting is for the benefit of the speaker. It spews without concern for how the words land or what impact the words have. This flies directly in the face of Ephesians 4:29. But what are we to do with all of these intense feelings and all of these offenses? We are to cast our cares upon

Christ (1 Peter 5:7). This is the pattern Christ himself laid out for us. Though he was sinned against daily during his earthly ministry, he went to his heavenly Father to be sustained while going to others to be an encouragement.

We should do likewise. When we speak, it ought to be for the benefit of the hearer, that we would give grace.

Power for Growth and Change

Just one chapter before Ephesians 4:29, the apostle Paul prays for those who read his words. His prayer reveals the required component to overcome our weaknesses in speech and in all other areas as well. Contained in that prayer, he says, "according to the riches of [God's] glory he may grant you to be strengthened with power through his Spirit in your inner being" (Ephesians 3:16).

Notice he doesn't pray that God would strengthen you according to how hard you try. He doesn't pray it would be according to the words your spouse deserves. This is how we act apart from Christ. But when we live our lives walking with Jesus, seeking to allow his word and his power to influence each moment of our lives, God strengthens us with power through the Holy Spirit "according to the riches of his glory." He gives wisdom and discernment to us that we do not possess when we are doing things on our own. He gives us words we would not naturally speak and causes those words to have greater effect than any we would conjure up.

God grants us his power because he delights when words are used according to his design. He does this because he loves you, and he loves your spouse. The result of this power from God is that "Christ may dwell in your hearts through faith" and that we would be "rooted and grounded in love" (Ephesians 3:17). The change we experience and the growth our spouse experiences in us come from the power of Christ at

23

work in our lives. Hope remains since the power for change is based on Christ and not on us.

Hope for the Butlers

This takes us back to the Butlers. When we look at the communication Tom and Marcy share in light of the four principles we just learned, it isn't hard to see the root of some of their problem. When they talk about intimacy, it seems God is far from their perspective, so naturally their words are far from God's design for them. They are not purposefully walking with Jesus in their speech, and they are experiencing the consequences of that.

What might happen in their marriage if Tom spoke so that Marcy encountered God in his speech? What would happen if Marcy built Tom up with her words instead of tearing him down? What would happen if they both spoke in a way fitting to the very sensitive occasion and committed to give grace with each word that passed through their lips?

The wonderful gift of speech comes with instructions and, in bold caps across the top, it reads "USE ONLY AS DIRECTED." Our willingness to adhere to those directions will reveal either wisdom or foolishness in our speech. Chapter 2 will help you evaluate how you're doing in this area.

Discussion/Reflection Questions

1. When you read 1 Peter 4:11, what areas of your communication do you feel need the most attention?

2. Which of the four principles seems to highlight your greatest area of need? What would need to occur for growth in that principle?

3. Think of a recent conflict in your marriage. How might that situation have been helped if principles 2, 3, and 4 had been applied? The more specific you are, the more helpful it will be.

4. Three specific pockets of time were mentioned: just before parting, just after coming back together, and around intimacy. If you could address just one, which would it be and what would be your first step?

5. It is important to track your own hope for change as you read and process this book. What three or four words would you use to describe your level of hope at this point?

Chapter 2

Looking into a Mirror

*Careless behavior puts a sword
into wicked men's hands to wound religion.*[1]
- Thomas Watson

*The words of a man's mouth are deep waters;
the fountain of wisdom is a bubbling brook.*
- Proverbs 18:4

All Quiet on the Domestic Front

Darryl and Linda Wilson were among the first members of
First Community Church. They've never been very active or
involved in the church, but with it just six minutes from their
house, it made sense for them to attend and to stay. They've
just celebrated their thirty-seventh wedding anniversary.

Life for the Wilsons has been steady with no "fire alarms."
However, over the years they have become detached from one
another. Gradually, Darryl has spent more time at work and
Linda has been happy to focus on the children at home. It
wasn't long until they were living separate lives. As the children grew, Linda found herself alone at ballet recitals and ball
games. On the weekends, Darryl found himself home alone
with the children as Linda floated from one errand to another,
avoiding as much time with Darryl as possible.

As time continued, their relationship was marked more by isolation than by closeness. And now, with the children gone, it feels like isolation is all they have left. They've drifted into being a couple that never really talks. It seems there's nothing for them to talk about. There was no great sin that one of them committed against the other. Just a thousand missed opportunities to build common interests and a life together.

Their isolation from one another is one of their best-kept secrets. On the surface, they seem like they're enjoying the empty-nest years. In reality, they're content to live separate lives for the remainder of their days. They stopped hoping for change a long time ago. *After all,* they think, *it's too late for anything to change.*

Perhaps you know some couples like the Wilsons. Perhaps you *are* the Wilsons. Can the silence ever be broken? Can healthy communication even exist after this many years of isolation?

The Problem Illustrated

It's not all that hard to see the folly in how the Wilsons built their marriage. Can you imagine what would happen to a sports team if teammates never communicated? How about a business where partners refused to communicate? We don't have to imagine because teams and businesses abound that have taken this approach. It's not pretty.

In such cases, wisdom fades into the background and folly takes over. Teams, businesses, and couples all lose sight of the bigger picture and suffer as a result. It's not unlike the man who kept tripping and became angry at his feet. He could punish those feet—drop books on them, refuse to put shoes on them in the scorching parking lot, or walk across a bed of nails. These things sure would punish his feet, but they wouldn't do a thing to address his clumsiness.

The Communication Connection

Among the many challenges the Wilsons face is acknowledging the reality that they've built a marriage that differs from God's design. They've acted in a way that disregards the role and authority of God. In their marriage they have lived as though there is no God. The Bible calls that manner of living, that manner of marriage, "foolish" (Psalm 14:1). Consequently, that makes Darryl and Linda foolish in their communication.

That may sound harsh to you, but the same is true of me and Gina. When we live as though God has not spoken, as though he has not promised good to us, as though his word does not exist, we are being fools. If we are going to grow in our communication and see grace in and through our marriage, we all must see where we are acting as fools so that we can lay those actions and attitudes aside and become wise.

Who among us likes to think of himself or herself as a fool? I venture to say no one. And yet, if we don't see the reality of our folly, we will never repent and seek change where change is necessary. We must face the reality that we act as fools far more often than we think; we must bypass our reflexive defenses and see it for what it is. The book of Proverbs helps us here. It doesn't name-call, though it's not afraid to be direct. (See, for example, Proverbs 1:7, 10:4, 14:3, 15:2) Often it takes an indirect approach to teach us wisdom. It doesn't outright call us fools; it shows us what folly is and leaves the diagnosis to us. This approach holds before us a mirror and asks us to judge for ourselves whether or not we are playing the part of a fool.

Seeing our folly can lead us to lose hope if we're not careful. The Bible looks at it quite differently. Seeing our folly is the beginning of hope since we will never turn in the right direction if we don't realize we're headed the wrong way. It takes humility to face our folly. It takes faith to see what we look like in the mirror of Proverbs 18. Remember: being a fool is not the end of the world; it is often the beginning of grace. The problem, the real danger, is in *staying* a fool. So let's understand how a fool behaves and seek to improve for the health of our marriages and for the glory of God.

Words Come from Our Hearts

To start our journey from folly to wisdom, from sin to repentance, we need an anchor. We need our own North Star so we we're not thrown off course by defensiveness or denial. One great place to start is in Proverbs 18:4: "The words of a man's mouth are deep waters; the fountain of wisdom is a bubbling brook."

Regardless of where we may fall on the "foolish/wise" continuum, Proverbs 18:4 provides a fixed reality: *our words reveal something deeper within us.* This shows our heart motivation. It includes our biases, our idols, our loves, our fears; it reveals all of them tied together. Words expose what is secretly concealed inside of us.

We learn from Matthew 12:34 that our words flow out of our hearts. We learn that out of the overflow of good treasure in our hearts will flow good words and out of the overflow of evil treasure will flow evil words. Because of this reality, we must own the words we say rather than make excuses for them.

If our words reveal sinful anger, we can't simply excuse those careless words as not being reflective of who we are and how we feel. Our words are deep waters. Nor can we cover the deep waters of our hearts by saying as few words as possible. In many counseling conversations, as I ask how someone feels about something or why he or she did something, I often get the answer, "I don't know." While I'm willing to concede that is an accurate answer some of the time, most of the time it is a cover that really says, *I don't want you to know how I feel about that or why I did that. Those waters are too deep to share with you, or they will overexpose me and I don't want that.* Should we expect people to hide from the ramifications of their words? Perhaps we should. But we should expect more from a Christian marriage.

Christian marriage is the joining together of two people into one flesh in fellowship with the Holy Spirit. It doesn't make any sense at all to keep the deeper parts of us separate and private from each other. They are to be shared, influenced by the other for the better, so that marital unity would grow. This occurs as couples use their words to bless and help. This occurs as couples commit to sharing for the glory of God. Then your marriage relationship will be marked by a healthy vulnerability.

What do your words reveal about the waters that run deep in your own soul? Do they reveal godliness deep within? Do they reveal selfishness or immaturity or bitterness or unhelpful independence from your spouse? Proverbs 18:4 says that what bubbles forth out of our mouths is directly related to what is percolating in our hearts. If we have a fountain of wisdom within us, then it will bubble over out of our mouths. However, if we have a cauldron of bitterness or selfishness deep within us, we should expect that to bubble forth instead.

This is the great challenge. It's not always easy to diagnose our own sin. It's particularly challenging to see our contribution to marital conflict if we see value and truth in what we say. An objective guide helps us know what we may otherwise never see. Proverbs continues to help us discover what we need to see on this journey. Let's continue walking the path laid out for us.

Understanding the Fool

One of the first things we learn about folly is what it says about God. Psalm 14:1 sums it up nicely for us.

The fool says in his heart, "There is no God."

Now, this is not necessarily a wholesale rejection of God by denying his existence. It could be the momentary, issue-by-issue denial of his authority. You may be faithful to your Bible reading plan and raise your hands during singing on Sundays (all with a genuine heart of worship), while still refusing to allow God to govern your speech. Though you are acting with wisdom in your study and your worship, you are a fool with your tongue.

The many areas where we may be walking rightly can cause us to be blind to the areas where we are walking wrongly. Or, put more directly, our many areas of wisdom can blind us to areas where we are still foolish. Do you see how elusive and deceptive folly can be?

Another important thing to learn is the inevitable outcome of folly. Because folly says "There is no God," the inevitable outcome of continuing in folly is hopelessness. Proverbs 10 has much to say about the fool, but one running theme is ruin. Continuing in folly not only ruins your life but deeply impacts those around you. Listen to this rapid-fire reality that Proverbs 10 lays down for us:

The wise of heart will receive commandments, but a babbling fool will come to ruin. (verse 8)

Whoever winks the eye causes trouble, and a babbling fool will come to ruin. (verse 10)

The wise lay up knowledge, but the mouth of a fool brings ruin near. (verse 14)

The lips of the righteous feed many, but fools die for lack of sense. (verse 21)

A husband or wife who continues in folly brings ruin into a marriage. It may not look like it right now in your marriage, but according to Scripture, folly always leads to ruin, to death, to destruction. People rarely knowingly walk on paths to destruction. They take those paths because they feel a degree of hope from them. Perhaps the beginning of the path is appealing. Perhaps a new path delivers them from a current path that is bitter or hard. Perhaps they are acting with instincts they've picked up throughout their lives or from their parents or friends.

The first step on any of these paths is the same, however. And if we could only learn to identify *that* step, we could protect ourselves from so much of the ruin we see in our marriages. What is that step? It is the step away from God. In order to take these paths toward destruction, we first must step away from God. And any step away from God is the step of a fool. Remember, a fool says in his heart, *There is no God.*

Are there paths you've been walking that have led to ruin? Are there patterns of communication or relating to your spouse that cause more pain than fruit? More hurt than help? It might just be possible that in those areas you've functionally rejected the leadership and help of God.

Foolishness has a pattern, a manner of life. The colors may change, the smells and flavors may vary. However, when folly is present, it shows up in similar ways. Proverbs 18 guides us on the next leg of the journey to diagnose the conduct of our lives. Let's learn from the fool so that we do not play the part of the fool.

Learning from the Fool

Together, we've made the case: if we are fools, it will show up in what we do. And, if we do the things that reveal folly, we surely must be foolish in those areas. As we return to Proverbs 18, we find at least four categories of folly that will provide a lens through which to look at our marriage, but mostly through which to look at ourselves.

1. Fools do not seek understanding.

The very first thing Proverbs 18 tells us about a fool is that he does not seek understanding. "A fool takes no pleasure in understanding, but only in expressing his opinion" (verse 2).

Guilty as charged. That was me at the beginning of our marriage. You may recall the introduction, where I described the horrific start we had to our marriage. Gina was struggling, and it was easier for me to judge her than it was to understand her struggles. It was easier to marginalize her challenges than it was to wrap my mind around them. It was easier not to seek understanding than to take responsibility for causing some of her challenges. I took no pleasure in understanding, but only in airing my own opinion.

Learning to seek understanding can be difficult. We first need to overcome our love of self and actually respect the opinions of others. If we assert our opinion without seeking to understand, we seem right in our own eyes. We may even win an argument. But we have not honored God, nor have we escaped folly.

Proverbs 20:5 counters the fool and holds up the course we all should take: "The purpose in a man's heart is like deep water, but a man of understanding will draw it out."

This is costly. This takes time. This requires trust and faith and patience. But lovingly seeking to understand one another leads to wisdom and to the marital harmony we need to honor God in our marriages. It benefits both husband and wife and nurtures healthy communication in marriage.

How might your marriage change if you were to seek understanding in an increasing way? How might that impact your communication? What fruit might your marital conversations produce if you made just this one adjustment? You could ask a question before coming to a conclusion. You could absorb a harsh tone by trying to understand where it's coming from.

Let me ask two more practical questions. What would need to happen for you to make this one change? What often gets in the way of achieving it? Let me propose one common obstacle, which also happens to be the next category of folly in Proverbs 18.

2. Fools rush to judgment.

Because a fool delights in airing his own opinion, he or she is very confident in his or her own judgments. Conflict emerges when a judgment is prematurely made or when there are two competing judgments. Someone feels wrongly accused. Someone is so confident of their understanding that they defend it. Look at how Proverbs 18:13 puts it: "If one gives an answer before he hears, it is his folly and shame."

As someone who does a fair amount of marriage counseling, I must tell you that an exciting part of my job is helping one spouse be heard and understood by the other spouse. Often there is a spouse whose judgments are set in stone. These foregone conclusions make listening akin to being underwater. No matter how carefully a spouse tries to share their judgments, the hearer's understanding is distorted and twisted by their own premature judgments.

Here are a few phrases I hear from people who have rushed to judgment before hearing the whole matter:

"I know what you're going to say."

"I hear you, but I know you don't mean it."

"Before you speak, let me just tell you how it is."

I hear a wife speak. The words are plain, and I understand what she has said. Then I ask the husband to repeat what he's just heard. And what he repeats doesn't sound a bit like what *I* just heard. We both listened to the same sounds come out of the wife's mouth, but what we understood is totally different. So, assuming I might have missed something, I ask the wife, "Is that what you meant?" And, of course, she says no. What is the difference? It is not *what* he is hearing, but *how* he is hearing it. It is not the words, but the understanding.

At times there are past experiences that influence the spouse's understanding, and I need to take the time as the counselor to learn about those past experiences. But usually I find that one of the spouses came to his or her unwavering opinion a long time earlier, and it has distorted conversations ever since. The repeated failure of proper understanding is what caused them to arrive in my office.

Was there a time early in your marriage when you had a hard conversation that created a judgment in you toward your spouse? Have you been listening through that lens ever since? Or perhaps it wasn't in your marriage at all. Perhaps it was a relationship you had prior to marriage, even with a sibling or parent. Is that judgment from the past coloring how you're communicating now? It is our own folly and shame to rush to judgment.

3. Fools look for a fight.

Another mark of folly in a person's life is how he or she is drawn to a fight. Sure, the offense or the statement or the event *could* be overlooked, but why overlook it if it can be confronted or contested? Look at how Proverbs 18:6–7 lays this out for us: "A fool's lips walk into a fight, and his mouth invites a beating. A fool's mouth is his ruin, and his lips are a snare to his soul."

If you're guilty of this on a regular basis, you are likely right now repeating excuses to justify yourself. *I'm just an honest person; I call it like I see it. Someone needs to teach him or her a lesson. If I don't say it, who will?* The excuses can be never ending, but the folly brings the same result: it generates conflict.

The model of Christian living and godly marriage calls us to a better way forward. Check out the following passages:

> Good sense makes one slow to anger, and it is his glory to overlook an offense. (Proverbs 19:11)

> Scoffers set a city aflame, but the wise turn away wrath. (Proverbs 29:8)

> Walk in a manner worthy of the calling to which you have been called, with all humility and gentleness, with patience, bearing with one another in love, eager to maintain the unity of the Spirit in the bond of peace. (Ephesians 4:1–3)

If we rightly understand marriage, what sense does it make to be in constant warfare with your spouse? As married couples, husbands and wives are one flesh and must nurture one another as their own flesh (Ephesians 5:29). Yet, when we foolishly love fighting, we set aflame our own households, we attack our spouse, and we attack our "one flesh" relationship. This leaves a wake of turmoil and destruction behind us.

If you love a fight, learn to love God more. If you find yourself in regular conflict with your spouse, turn away from focusing first on why he or she deserved it and focus first on your own propensity toward it. In this way, you will honor God and avoid ruining your marriage with your own tongue.

4. Fools sow discord.

I'm not a handyman by any stretch, but I will attempt minor repairs around our house. There are two types of projects I really don't like taking on—plumbing and electrical. A mistake in these areas holds the potential for so much damage. In each case, the process is similar. You shut off the water or electricity. Then you do your work. But you don't yet have any idea if you've done your work correctly. You must first turn the water or electricity back on. You can only tell your success or failure by looking at the result.

Pause now and consider carefully the people around you—your spouse, children, and coworkers. What is the result of your words in their lives? Generally speaking, are they glad you spoke? Did your words have a positive effect on them?

We learned earlier in this chapter that words come from deep within. Proverbs 18:8 tells us that our words also go deep within the hearer. It says, "The words of a whisperer are like delicious morsels; they go down into the inner parts of the body."

Have you ever experienced the disproportionate effect of words? Sometimes, a small and simple kindness is expressed and it multiplies its joy throughout your day. Sometimes, a small and thoughtless critique is shared, which ruins your weekend. Why? It is because words go deep. Paraphrasing

Thomas Watson (see opening quote), words in a fool's mouth are like swords, inflicting injury on marriage. Each whisper, each ill-intended word penetrates like a sword until all affection and unity is slain, leaving no love left for a marriage to function. In this way, fools sow discord.

Summing It All Up

Proverbs 18:20–21 gets to the heart of the matter. If we fail to understand and embrace what these verses say, we will totally miss the sources of our communication problems and continue in the way of the fool. Read carefully: "From the fruit of a man's mouth his stomach is satisfied; he is satisfied by the yield of his lips. Death and life are in the power of the tongue, and those who love it will eat its fruits."

Lips generate a harvest. Which kind of harvest you reap is determined by which kinds of words are sown into the soil of your marriage. The words sown into our marriages flow out of the intentions of our hearts. If you've sown wisely, you're likely experiencing a harvest of kindness and mercy and acceptance and love and hope. If you've sown foolishly in your marriage, your harvest is likely bitterness and conflict and tumult and isolation and sadness. Yet, even if you've sown in this way for decades, hope is not lost.

Power for Growth and Change

In Romans 7, Paul writes a personal testimony. He wants to do right, but regularly does wrong. His life is marked by a desire to obey but a legacy of falling short, a harvest of brokenness and disappointments.

Perhaps as you looked into the mirror that Proverbs 18 held up to you, you saw patterns of folly. Perhaps you were discouraged. Perhaps you were disheartened. Perhaps you join Paul as he arrives at his self-diagnosis: "Wretched man that I am! Who will deliver me from this body of death?" (Romans 7:24).

Notice Paul does not say, "Wretched man that I am! What must I do to deliver myself from this body of death?" Nor does he say, "Wretched spouse that I have! Who will deliver me from this marriage?" Paul realized he could not dig more deeply into himself to find the power to overcome the folly trapped within. If there was going to be hope for people like Paul, for people like us, it would have to come from someone delivering us.

Paul's answer to his seemingly hopeless question is first found in Romans 7:25, "Thanks be to God through Jesus Christ our Lord!" Then he expounds upon this in what is considered one of the most glorious chapters in all of Scripture, Romans 8.

Hope for the fool is found in Jesus. It is found in the removal of condemnation (Romans 8:1), in adoption as sons and daughters (Romans 8:15), and in supernatural help provided by the Spirit (Romans 8:26). We finally discover that nothing in all of creation, not even our folly, can separate us from hope in Christ. This is good news for us, and it is good news for the Wilsons.

Hope for the Wilsons

Darryl and Linda have built foolishly for thirty-seven years. What is the point of changing things now? What hope is there?

The Wilsons have hope because you and I have hope. Remember that Jesus came not to call the righteous, but sinners. (See Matthew 9:12–13.) He came and died for husbands like Darryl. He now lives for wives like Linda. Remember, being a fool is not the end of the world; realizing our folly is often the beginning of grace. The problem, the real danger, is in *staying* a fool.

Brother or sister, we fools have a glorious Savior. And our current folly may just be the stage of Jesus's next miracle. Do you want to see his power at work in your marriage? Do you want to be transformed so that your words are wise and good? Are you tired of harvesting the fruit of folly that you've sown into your marriage?

Jesus is the way. Wisdom is the means. And a healthy combination of humility and faith is the currency. The next chapter provides much needed instruction for the fool who desires to become wise.

Discussion/Reflection Questions

1. How do you relate to the idea of being foolish? Do you identify with it? Do you feel condemned by it? Do you repel it or reject it? Why?

2. What do you believe are the influences that have most shaped your use of words? Does the answer to that question reveal something new to you?

3. Which of the four headings under "Learning from the Fool" seems closest to the challenges you bring to your marital communication? Which seems least like you? Explain.

4. In what ways should we be encouraged by Christ delivering us from our folly? List several and share how they can be encouraging.

5. How can you find comfort when your folly is revealed? How does your folly position you for receiving grace from God?

Chapter 3

Taming the Tongue

*God cares about your mouth. God cares about your lips
and your tongue. He cares about what goes in, but he
cares a lot more about what comes out (Matthew 15:11).
So I think what God means to do...is to help you become
the kind of person whose mouth will freely, refreshingly
bring forth more and more life for other people.
God wants to make your mouth a fountain of life.*[1]

\- John Piper

*Whoever keeps his mouth and his tongue
keeps himself out of trouble.*

\- Proverbs 21:23

The War of the Joneses

Bill and Shirley Jones have been married for seven years,
though they were engaged for three years prior to their wedding and had been an on-again-off-again couple for the six
years prior to that. They've never wanted to be with anyone
other than each other, but conflict has always been the pre-
dominant theme of their relationship. That was the primary
reason behind their multiple breakups in the early years.

When it comes to communication, they're almost never
on the same page. One small disagreement tends to erupt into
deep offense and conflict. Their voices elevate, their pulses

race, their faces redden, and the tensions mount, lingering long in the aftermath of each conflict. With the addition of two young children, there's been even more cause for conflict and more cause for concern when their yelling frightens the kids.

Privately, they regret the way they talk to each other. They know they've used their words to harm one another and to serve their own agendas. What's worse, they know there are better ways to communicate, but they simply can't get there. Separately, they've often resolved to do better, only to fall into anger and conflict yet again.

They've pulled back from friends and only attend their small group at First Community Church sporadically because they want to hide this part of their marriage. As a result, no one really knows the degree of conflict or brokenness in their relationship. The War of the Joneses has taken a significant toll on Bill and Shirley. They're discouraged and disheartened, feeling stuck without a way out.

Perhaps you know some couples like the Joneses. Perhaps you are the Joneses. Is there hope? Will they ever get beyond war and find peace?

The Problem Illustrated

There is a legend surrounding Alexander the Great, the renowned Greek warrior who conquered the world known to him in the 300s BC. The legend focuses on him as a boy when he first met his great horse, Bucephalus. (What good is a marital communication book if it doesn't have a good horse story?)

Bucephalus was large and wild. In fact, his trainer considered him untamable. Due to his wild nature and his massive presence, he was a danger to all who came near him. When Alexander's father, King Phillip II, saw how this horse behaved, he wanted no part of him. Then young Alexander stepped in. He offered to pay for the horse himself if he could not tame him. One thing led to another and Alexander tamed the great beast, upon whose back he led conquest after conquest.

This chapter addresses your "Bucephalus"—your tongue. Taming the tongue is the presenting need for the Joneses and a regular need in all marriages. James guides this next step of the journey, providing large-print warning labels as well as easy-to-understand user instructions.

The Communication Connection

In chapter one, we addressed the role of the heart in communication; it is the overflowing source of the words we speak. Here, we cover the other side of that transaction. Words *start* in the heart; they flow out of the mouth. So we are called to bring the tongue under submission, to tame it rather than allow it to run wild.

When it comes to taming the tongue, we first must admit we have a problem. This problem is captured in James 3:9-10.

> With [the tongue] we bless our Lord and Father, and with it we curse people who are made in the likeness of God. From the same mouth come blessing and cursing. My brothers, these things ought not to be so.

And that is where we start.

We Have a Problem

When it comes to actors in our time, I believe Tom Hanks is among the best. In addition to his memorable performances, he has a collection of stand-out lines: "Life is like a box of chocolates" and "There's a snake in my boot." But perhaps none fits our next point more than one of his lines from Apollo 13: "Houston, we have a problem." Those words triggered fear in the crew of Apollo 13. However, they also triggered the best minds the nation could assemble to work on the problem. Realizing they had a problem was the pivotal first step in moving toward a solution.

When it comes to communication, we all have a problem: our tongues. Since we belong to God both body and soul, and since he himself is Lord of all, then all of who we are and all of what we are belong to God, including our speech. We have been freed from the power of sin and don't need to walk in it any longer. But the believers James was addressing were not living that way. They were using their words for both blessing and cursing. James says it simply: "these things ought not to be so" (3:10).

We may craft our excuses and try to push back from James's teaching. We may be uncomfortable that he doesn't give us the wiggle room we prefer, particularly in our marital conversations. However, we are better off if we just admit and embrace the fact that we have a problem. It's okay to admit it; in fact, it is necessary. It is the first step toward health and healing. It is the step we all must take as we embrace and believe the gospel of Christ. Our tongues are a problem. Fact. Settled. Resolved.

How did the tongue become such a danger? Well, let's retrace James's thought process from the beginning of chapter three as he sets the stage.

As the Tongue Goes, So Goes the Person

James lays out the situation this way:

> If we put bits into the mouths of horses so that they obey us, we guide their whole bodies as well. Look at the ships also: though they are so large and are driven by strong winds, they are guided by a very small rudder wherever the will of the pilot directs. So also

the tongue is a small member, yet it boasts of great things (3:3–5).

These verses hardly require an explanation. The smallest piece of the machine (the bit for the horse and the rudder for the ship) steers the entire thing. Through the power of the small bit, the massive beast is controlled. Through the power of the small rudder, the massive ship is directed. So it is in verse 5 with people: though the tongue is a small part of the body, it is able to boast of great control and influence.

This is not a condition we overcome; it is a fact we must embrace. The power of our words is not something we outgrow. It is something we acknowledge so we can surrender control of our words to God. Proverbs 21:23 shows us that if we purpose to tame the tongue, then the whole of us is kept out of trouble:

Whoever keeps his mouth and his tongue keeps himself out of trouble.

It should be said that the tongue is not the only way we find trouble, but it is among the biggest culprits in creating trouble, for the speaker and hearers alike. How many marital conflicts could be avoided if we simply avoided saying *that*? How many disappointments could have been avoided if we had simply said *this*? How many marriages would still exist, and exist joyfully, if one or both spouses kept themselves out of trouble by watching what they said? Our words are powerful indeed.

Yet, we use this power for evil as well as good. We use our words to manipulate as well as encourage. We use them to tear down and we use them to build up. We use words to curse those made in God's image as well as to bless the Maker of those we're cursing. As we survey the aftermath in our own lives, we discover the harsh reality—the duality of our words leaves mass destruction in its wake.

Weapon of Mass Destruction

I don't know what comes into your mind when you hear the words "weapons of mass destruction." Perhaps it is the voice of George W. Bush in the midst of the controversy of the Iraq War. Perhaps it is the WWII bombing of Hiroshima and Nagasaki. Regardless of what comes to mind, it's all kind of awful, isn't it? Weapons of mass destruction are massively destructive.

Is it a surprise to discover that you have one of these weapons of mass destruction trapped behind your teeth and in your throat? The bit and rudder that steer the machine of your life contain the potential to wreak havoc in the lives of others. James continues to lay out his case:

> So also the tongue is a small member, yet it boasts of great things… And the tongue is a fire, a world of unrighteousness. The tongue is set among our members, staining the whole body, setting on fire the entire the course of life, and set on fire by hell. (3:5–6)

James exhorts us to beware that our words set aflame forests and defile the entire body. Even beyond that, they hold the power to set on fire our entire course for life. You may be thinking now of people in your past against whom you've spoken or who have spoken against you. You're thinking of the devastation you've experienced as a result of others, and the damage that you've created for others. Right now as you sit at your desk or on your sofa or lie in your bed, you are testifying to the danger that lies in the tongue.

Comfort for us in our regret or sorrow is coming, but that's not where James goes next. Right when we could use some encouragement, James doubles down on the problem and makes the picture even bleaker. Can this tongue be tamed? Let's let him answer:

> For every kind of beast and bird, of reptile and sea creature, can be tamed and has been tamed by mankind, but no human being can tame the tongue. It is a restless evil, full of deadly poison. (3:7–8)

So we find that we're stuck with a poisonous, fiery, restless weapon that wreaks havoc on our lives and the lives of those around us. It risks the welfare of those we love and those we don't even know. There is no taming it, regardless of the amount of human effort. Our tongues will destroy, and our tongues will betray us. We have no power to stop it. But God, in his grace, doesn't let this word be the end of the story.

As the Person Goes, So Goes the Tongue

Ephesians 2:4 has one of my favorite phrases in all of Scripture: "But God." Often the Scriptures take us face-to-face with the hopeless reality of our human condition. James 3 is no exception. We stand there, at the end of a dark alley with nothing but impenetrable walls surrounding us and we are hopeless. We realize we have no resources to deal with what has transpired, and we are trapped, destined to fail.

Then hope arrives. It arrives not in the form of self-discovery but self-abandonment. It arrives not in our own strength but in the fruit and power of the Spirit. It arrives not because of us but because of God. Look at the rest of the sentence from Ephesians 2:4–7:

But God, being rich in mercy, because of the great love with which he loved us, even when we were dead in our trespasses, made us alive together with Christ—by grace you have been saved—and raised us up with him and seated us with him in the heavenly places in Christ Jesus, so that in the coming ages he might show the immeasurable riches of his grace in kindness toward us in Christ Jesus.

I am not going to take all of that glorious truth apart in this chapter. I will simply make a few observations. First, we were dead. That is a hopeless condition. Second, God himself made us alive. Third, he did it by grace. Fourth, he did it to show the surpassing riches of his grace in kindness toward us in Christ Jesus. Our hopelessness was conquered because God conquered us. He overcame our biggest problem and gave us hope. He gave us power. He gave us life.

James 3 continues with some questions that illustrate his point:

Does a spring pour forth from the same opening both fresh and salt water? Can a fig tree, my brothers, bear olives, or a grapevine produce figs? Neither can a salt pond yield fresh water. (verses 11–12)

A fountain can only send out one type of water and a fig tree can only produce one kind of fruit. If you want to change the product, you must first change the source. James has told us we can't accomplish this on our own. At first this sounds like bad news, but it is actually wonderful for us.

God, being rich in mercy, has shown his kindness toward you in Christ (Ephesians 2:4–5). You were dead but now you are alive in Christ. Once you were not his, but now you are his.

Once you had not received mercy, but now you have received mercy (1 Peter 2:10). And with his kindness comes the presence and power of his Spirit. This is why Piper declares,

> God cares about your mouth. God cares about your lips and your tongue. He cares about what goes in, but he cares a lot more about what comes out (Matthew 15:11). So I think what God means to do…is to help you become the kind of person whose mouth will freely, refreshingly bring forth more and more life for other people. God wants to make your mouth a fountain of life.[2]

God is in the business of changing hearts, of changing people. He has little interest in redeeming tongues only. He goes after the man, the woman, knowing that once the man or woman truly belongs to him, the tongue is sure to follow. Marriages need husbands and wives who are conquered by God. When God conquers a husband and wife, he conquers their hearts, their minds, and their tongues.

The tongue is powerful; the Spirit is more so. The tongue has great influence; the Spirit of God has more (see 1 Corinthians 4:20). The tongue sets the forest ablaze in destruction; the Spirit sets the heart ablaze unto life and victory and good. This allows us to say in the end, "All glory be to Christ!"

Dealing with Our Forked Tongues

Oh, if we could only remain there. If we could just worship and thank God for what he's done. But we must be a people who go from the heights of magnificent theology to the depths of very practical and honest application. Life is now lived in the already / not yet. We already have the fullness of the Spirit to help and change us. We are not yet perfected by his work, but we are already fully redeemed. We are not yet fully glorified.

So we acknowledge that both fresh and salt water flow from our fountains. We admit that both figs and olives grow on our trees. We know we speak with a forked tongue, sometimes praising and sometimes cursing. We hear the echo of James's words resounding in our convicted hearts, "My brothers, these things ought not to be so" (3:10).

Here, truth must prevail. If you are in Christ, you *are* an overcomer. If God has called you his, you *do* have the power of the Spirit within you. When talking about his own suffering, Paul declared,

> Him we proclaim, warning everyone and teaching everyone with all wisdom, that we may present everyone mature in Christ. For this I toil, struggling *with all his energy* that he powerfully works within me. (Colossians 1:28–29, emphasis mine)

So that we may be mature in Christ, we must press on with all *his* energy to bring our tongue under *his* authority. We are not fatalistic, believing there is no hope. We are exclusive, believing that our only hope is Christ. We do not lie down and surrender to this small member. We stand and fight in the great power of our divine advocate. How do we do this? We fight on many fronts.

Devotional work

We start by tending to our own relationship with Christ (John 15:1–11). It is the most important work we can do for our marriages. If we are going to toil in *his* energy and live under *his* authority, we will need to know what he says and what he calls us to do. This can be done best as we come to his word and read what he's revealed there. Of course, we must work on our relationship with our spouse. But if we skip this devotional work, we will inevitably run into our own shortcomings and weaknesses and our tongues will outrun our ability to control them. Knowing Christ well is the first necessary step in dealing with the problem of our words.

Proactive work

We live aware of the problem between our hearts and our tongues, and we don't wait for an epic failure before we address it. We take action (James 1:22–25). We memorize passages of Scripture that specifically address our struggle so that the verses are always with us, sheathed and ready for battle whenever the need arises. In this way, we are never confronted with temptation as unarmed soldiers. We always stand at the ready.

We commit to a regular intake of resources that focus on speech. Perhaps it is a Christian podcast or your favorite preacher. Perhaps it is a book on speech or holiness or communication. Perhaps it's rereading this book annually. We keep this as an ongoing prayer request and discuss it in our accountability groups. Then we embrace the wise counsel James offered in James 1: we speak slowly with God's help, allowing wisdom to catch up with our lips.

Repenting work

Even as we work proactively, we are bound to stumble and fall. That is not the time to pick up your ball and go home. That is the time to repent. What does this look like?

You acknowledge truth for what it is. You refuse to allow excuses or explanations to nullify or negate any of the guilt that comes from true conviction. You acknowledge your wrongdoing, your sin, and you repent. "Sounds good, Rob, but what does that even look like?" Glad you asked.

Repenting begins with acknowledging that your actions have been out of line with the will of God, but it doesn't stop there. Once you see the truth, you seek out those who have been affected by your sin. You speak with specificity and ask for their forgiveness. But it doesn't stop there. There is more.

Biblical repentance requires a "turning from" one thing and a "turning to" another (Ephesians 4:22–24). This is what the word *repent* means. Repentance isn't complete until you cycle back to your proactive work. You turn from your sinful speech toward a life that is Christ-oriented. This reactive work is essential if you hope to sin less through your speech. The faith and humility required in doing reactive work is where God builds powerful saints who grow in holiness.

Community work

Do you remember our Apollo 13 scenario: "Houston, we have a problem"? There was no chance those men in the ship were going to solve the problem on their own. The many NASA experts on the ground needed to work together with the crew in order for the module to reach earth safely. In the same way, we must do community work. Yes, we need proactive work. We need repenting work. But we also must do community work. I'm talking about marital community, family community, small group community, and even work community if appropriate.

We share with those around us that we desire to grow in how we use our tongues. We make this an area of special focus in our marriages. We ask the family for their help in pointing out when our speech is not helpful to them. We involve a pastor or friend. And then comes the hardest part of all—we listen to and believe them when they give us input. We don't bite them when they extend a hand of help to us. We assume any disagreement is because we don't see *ourselves* accurately, not because *they* don't see *us* accurately.

You'd be surprised how many folks could and would desire to walk with you through this battle. You'd also be surprised how many are walking through the same battle. I feel confident in assuming that the majority of your community is populated with people who have tongues. If they have one, then they know the battle because their tongues cannot be tamed either.

The paradigm of "devotional/proactive/repenting/community work" is one that will serve you in the battle against any area of sin. This is not exclusive to sins of speech, but oh how helpful it is when fighting sins of the tongue.

Power for Growth and Change

Jesus knows our need to be in relationship with him. He knows our propensity toward selfishness as we destroy the very thing we hope to build. In John 15, Jesus gives one of his most memorable illustrations to reveal the glorious fruit that comes from a relationship with him, while also illustrating the hopelessness of living apart from him.

> Abide in me, and I in you. As the branch cannot bear fruit by itself, unless it abides in the vine, neither can you, unless you abide in me. I am the vine; you are the branches. Whoever abides in me and I in him, he it is that bears much fruit, for apart from me you can do nothing. (15:4–5)

Each morning, and then many times throughout the day, we check our connection to the vine. Am I planning my day in such a way that Jesus can be seen in my actions, my meetings, my words, and my behavior? As you call one another throughout the day, do you purpose to honor Christ in each conversation? When challenging topics come up, do you first remember that you are connected to Christ? When you see bad fruit (conflict, hurt, offense, etc.), are you quick to blame your spouse or do you look to your vine-connection?

Unless the life of the vine is flowing into the branches of our lives, we will not bear good fruit. Cut flowers are beautiful to be sure, but they've been separated from the vine or tree or bush. They've been separated from the very thing that brings them life. Even as they look pretty they are in the act of dying. This is what happens to the husband or wife that seeks to walk apart from Christ.

But if we walk with Christ, if we nurture our relationship with him so that what he loves is what we love most, and what he hates is what we hate most, we will see great things happen in and through our communication. Jesus stated it later in the chapter: "As the Father has loved me, so have I loved you. Abide in my love" (verse 9). Christ must be the constant centerpiece in our lives. We need it. And the Joneses need it.

Hope for the Joneses

Will our friends Bill and Shirley ever be able to achieve peace? Will their hearts ever allow their tongues to function in the way we've just learned? They've learned to fight and hurt in order to get their way. Is it possible for them to learn another way? Can they adapt, turning away from their destructive habits of conflict and turning instead to a godly way of communication? Thus far, they've missed out on the great peace and fruit God has for them. He has blessing and strength and wholeness and joy and health for Bill and Shirley. And he desires that for you too.

Under the influence of the Spirit's power, our words bring healing. Our tongues bring hope. Our lips deliver good news. Our words reveal life. Let me ask you, do you love Christ? Do you mean to follow him for the remainder of your days? If so, then speak in a manner worthy of your calling (Ephesians 4:1). Join the ranks of Christians throughout the ages and dispense some of the grace you've received from the Father.

Your spouse will thank you. Your kids will thank you. Your boss and coworkers will thank you. But allow me to take it one step further. As your tongue is tamed in the power of the Spirit, you will experience the pleasure of your heavenly Father.

Discussion/Reflection Questions

1. What excuses have you used to give your tongue wiggle room? Be honest and share the ones you've used the most.

2. Think of a recent conflict. Did you say something you wish you could take back? Was there a moment you'd like to do over? How might the conflict have changed if you paused before speaking?

3. How does the mercy of God impact the way you use your tongue? Be specific?

4. Which of the four kinds of work (devotional, proactive, repenting, community) seems most important for you to address? How about as a couple?

5. What are one or two things that most interfere with your "connection" to Jesus? How can you address these things to improve your connection to the vine?

Section 2:

Tools for Communication

WITH A SOLID foundation in Christ and an understanding laid down for us from the Scriptures, we turn our attention to application. We're repeatedly reminded that we must not settle for knowledge alone. Knowledge alone doesn't help us grow or cause our marriage to thrive. Knowledge, left to itself, puffs up and convinces us we've done something when we haven't yet done anything.

You can study physiology and exercise science. You can fill your garage with the best gym equipment. You can purchase coordinating shorts, shirts, and sneakers to look like a million bucks. And none of it will do you any good if you don't use it. You will not lose the weight or gain the muscle you desire. You will not experience the benefits of exercise by studying it alone. You actually need to start using the equipment. The same is true of knowledge. We need to take our knowledge and work it out (Philippians 2:12).

This section contains five key tools for communication. I've seen them have great effect for couples as they are applied with faith and consistency. Their foundation is in Scripture and they flow out of life experience.

Read these chapters carefully, taking note of any place you are inclined to push back. If there are any places where you distance yourself from the content, those may be the very places you should look to start applying the tools. And if you are tired, weary of trying, and don't think you'll be able to find the faith to keep fighting for healthy communication, pause and pray. God wants to draw near and help, and he promises that those who keep doing good will reap if they don't lose heart (Galatians 6:9).

As you read, don't take these tools simply at face value. I'll use examples and illustrations throughout, but make these tools your own. Adapt them to work within the culture and dynamics of your marriage. Don't just read them. Don't just learn them. Use them.

Discussion/Reflection Questions

Preparing for Section Two

1. In the discussion questions from chapter 1, you were asked to track how hopeful you are for change. After learning some of our fundamental problems and that Jesus provides the answer, how is your hope right now? Rate it on a scale from 1 to 10.

2. Identify one or two particular patterns of challenge you face in your marital communication. What are they and what normally happens when those moments occur?

3. Do you normally take instruction from others well? Do you normally push against it?

Throughout this section, keep in mind how you've answered these questions and seek to receive these tools well.

Chapter 4

The Tool of First Response

*It is our choices…that show what we truly are,
far more than our abilities.*[1]
- J. K. Rowling

*A soft answer turns away wrath,
but a harsh word stirs up anger.*
- Proverbs 15:1

FIRST RESPONDERS ARE some of the bravest among us. These are the firefighters, police, and EMTs who serve in our communities and come when we call. When there is danger or crisis, those who respond first face the greatest risk to their own well-being. We are a safer and better society because of them. Those of you who serve in this way, thank you!

There are first responders of a different kind at work in our communication. Each day in many ways we are acted upon. Perhaps we are the recipients of random acts of kindness. Likely, we are also recipients of random acts of rudeness. And certainly we are daily recipients of purposeful acts of sin.

As sin recipients, we sometimes feel like the course of events is set. *She said something nasty. He did something selfish. She snapped at me. He raised his voice. What else am I supposed to do? After all, they started it!* You've been there before. You know this feeling. But I have a tool that can protect you from this knee-jerk reaction.

I call it the tool of first response. Just when we feel a situation is forced upon us, this tool flies in, cape flapping in the wind, and rescues us from our fatalism. It returns us to faith-filled, empowered hope. It's quite simple: *The course of a conflict is determined by the person who responds, not the one who initiates.*

Wait a minute. What? How can that be? How can it be that someone picking a fight doesn't decide whether or not they get one? How can it be that someone being nasty doesn't necessarily get "nasty" thrown back at them? After all, that's what they have coming to them, isn't it? Let's take a look at this tool in action by studying Jesus himself.

Jesus as First Responder

We find the powerful story in Luke 20. Once again, Jesus's teaching has offended and enraged the Pharisees. They're ready to get physical with their displeasure, but they're afraid of the crowd's response. Here is the story:

> The scribes and the chief priests sought to lay hands on him at that very hour, for they perceived that he had told this parable against them, but they feared the people. So they watched him and sent spies, who pretended to be sincere, that they might catch him in something he said, so as to deliver him up to the authority and jurisdiction of the governor. So they asked him, "Teacher, we know that you speak and teach rightly, and show no partiality, but truly teach the way of God. Is it lawful for us to give tribute to Caesar, or not?" But he perceived their craftiness, and said to them, "Show me a denarius. Whose likeness

and inscription does it have?" They said, "Caesar's." He said to them, "Then render to Caesar the things that are Caesar's, and to God the things that are God's." And they were not able in the presence of the people to catch him in what he said, but marveling at his answer they became silent. (20:19–26)

The hunters had their prey in their sights and were set to pounce. They laid down their trap: *"Let's ask a question that will cause him to turn the crowd against him, no matter how he answers."* The plan was simple, clean, and foolproof. The trap was set in stone. That is, until Jesus responded.

His response to their insidious ambush redirected the conversation, robbed them of their prey, and serves to this day as a blessing to all who ponder its meaning. Brilliant! Incredible! But this was more than a momentary flash of skill; he regularly diffused arguments through his redemptive responses.

In Matthew 12, Jesus's grand claims and controversial preaching embarrassed his family. They sought to pull him from the public eye. He was told they wanted to talk with him. In the same situation, you and I might have excused ourselves, pulling away from the crowd to defend what we were doing. We would have argued or called attention to the banality of their lives compared to ours. But Jesus as first responder, unwavering in his message, converted their request into another timeless lesson. "Whoever does the will of my Father in heaven is my brother and sister and mother" (verse 50).

In Luke 23, Pilate is interrogating Jesus as he determines Jesus's fate. From his lofty place of power, Pilate asks "Are you the King of the Jews?" Jesus could simply have said yes. That would have ended the conversation and satisfied Pilate's curiosity. But that was not best for Pilate, because Pilate had a bigger problem than determining what to do with Jesus. Pilate was lost and needed to deal with the state of his own soul. Jesus as first responder said, "You have said so." Less clear, a bit enigmatic, and definitely not what Pilate was looking for. However, it was exactly what Pilate needed. Even in the intensity of this trial, Jesus was redirecting conversations, wresting them from the hand of the aggressor to steer them toward redemptive purposes.

The pattern continues over and over again. Those who schemed against him failed time and again because the power to decide the direction of each conflict rested with Jesus, the first responder. Lest we believe this was just a skill that the God-Man possessed, it turns out it works for normal people like us too.

A soft answer turns away wrath, but a harsh word stirs up anger. (Proverbs 15:1)

Any confusion surrounding this tool is not because we don't understand it. The command and the premise are clear: we are to respond redemptively, even when the initial action taken toward us is ungodly. There is little doubt in my mind that if married couples regularly practiced this one proverb, most of their conflicts would go away.

The implications of this command, of following Jesus's example, were huge for our marriage relationship. Gina's sin did not give me free license to sin in return. And conversely, my sin did not give her free license either. The principle captured in the tool of first response called us to take a poorly spoken comment, a sharp verbal dagger, and redirect it. Turn it to Christ. Direct it away from division and toward unity. To pull this off, we needed help. (For the record, we *still* need help.) And you'll need help, too. Thankfully, help is being offered.

God as First Responder to Us

Perhaps the example of Christ is a bit abstract for you. Perhaps Proverbs 15:1 is a hard concept to apply in your context. Are you aware that you already receive "first responder" grace? What is more, you receive it from someone who has every right to judge you and hold you accountable for your every action, word, and thought. Redemptive first responding is how God relates to you every day!

God's responses to us are always for our good (Psalm 119:68). They are not according to our sins, but according to his steadfast love (Psalm 25:7). He is not vengeful toward us, nor does he repay us for our iniquities (Psalm 103:10). Paul muses on this theme when he writes:

> For by grace you have been saved through faith. And this is not your own doing; it is the gift of God, not a result of works, so that no one may boast. (Ephesians 2:8–9)

In our rebellion against God, we do not deserve grace. In fact, the idea of deserving grace is oxymoronic. Nor do we ever earn grace, as though God was compelled to save and adopt us. No, our salvation is a gift. Our being preserved in our walk with Christ is a daily grace we receive. It is not because you figured it out and others did not. Hosea 2:23 puts it this way: "I will have mercy on No Mercy, and I will say to Not My People, 'You are my people.'"

We looked earlier at the wonderful example we have in Christ as he responded to the Pharisees. But our thinking must not stop with how undeservedly wronged he was by the Pharisees or the Roman soldiers. He was undeservedly wronged by you and by me. Our sin was grievous and deserving of eternal death. However, not even that magnitude of sin could confine him to treating us harshly. No, in the face of blatant sin committed against him, he gives us his righteousness and forgiveness, turning our relationship away from judgment and toward redemption. Then, with immeasurable mercy and grace, he grants his Spirit to empower us to act accordingly.

> Therefore, my beloved, as you have always obeyed, so now, not only as in my presence but much more in my absence, work out your own salvation with fear and trembling, for it is God who works in you, both to will and to work for his good pleasure. (Philippians 2:12–13)

The course of our war with God was set. We were his enemies, children of wrath, separated from Christ, without hope and without God (Ephesians 2). But God changed the conversation; he redirected our relationship. He made us alive with Christ out of his immeasurable depths of mercy. He then gives us his grace to extend to others.

When our spouse sins against us, our fleshly response is to sin back, to get even. But this is not of God and has no place in a Christian marriage. Rather, we ought to respond as one who has received far more grace than we'll ever be called to extend. We ought to act out of our love for God, out of our gratitude for his love and grace, to redirect the conversation toward one of redemption and mercy.

Why Is This So Hard for Us?

With such clear directions and such clear examples, why do we still find this so hard? Why don't we just respond with grace and enjoy the fruit it produces in our marriages and in our homes?

At this point, we have to get honest with one another. We have to put down the abstractions and the platitudes and look at ourselves in the mirror. There are a few common reasons this is hard for us, but we'll never overcome them if we're afraid to face them. So, with courage in our hearts and our eyes on the grace given to us in Christ, let's look at some reasons this is so hard.

We just don't want to do it.

It is hard to give grace because often we just don't want to. It doesn't seem fair to give grace when we've been hurt so badly. In fact, sometimes the thought is so far from our minds that we don't even think of grace as a possible response.

"Turning the other cheek" seems great when you read it in the Bible, but it seems almost farcical when trying to live it out. How does one get struck in the face (or in the heart) and turn, asking for another? We can teach our children to "overlook an offense," but when it's our turn to do it, the pain and frustration are too great even to conceive of allowing an offense to go unaddressed. The tool of first response is hard because we just don't want to use it.

We are no good at obedience.

At a deeper level, this is hard because we're not accustomed to living as disciples. Often our faith is lived out on our terms, and we are not pressed to obey. If we don't like the decision our pastor makes, we may just leave and find another church. If we don't like the attitude of our boss, we may leave and find another job. If we don't like the behavior of our spouse, we may leave and find another one.

Our struggle with obedience is part of being human. It started with our first parents, Adam and Eve, who proved they were not good at obeying. It was passed down through the ages to you and to me. We love our own preferences and getting our own way. This selfishness drives us to leave rather than stay, to accuse rather than love, and to defend rather than receive. It is the opposite of how Jesus responded. Obedience isn't natural to us. We need Jesus every day if we are going to respond like he does.

We don't know how to respond this way.

Since we're not accustomed to living this way, we can be unprepared and ill-equipped when called to do so. The point of temptation comes, and we don't have the tools necessary to navigate conflict to the glory of God. All we're left with is our own effort and wisdom, and that's not much. In those moments, we forget just how equipped we truly are. We forget what God has already shown us. We forget to turn to God and act in his power. We must remember how frequently the Scriptures speak to these things. You've already read Proverbs 15:1, which reveals that we are not powerless when someone's wrath is headed our way. Here are some more passages:

- Proverbs 16:7 – "When a man's ways please the Lord, he makes even his enemies to be at peace with him."
  - *This verse tells us there's a connection between our own conduct and the measure of peace or conflict that surrounds us.*
- Matthew 18:15 – "If your brother sins against you, go and tell him his fault, between you and him alone. If he listens to you, you have gained your brother."
  - *When we're sinned against, the restoration of the brother is far more important than any broadcasting of his or her action against you.*

> *Taking care of it privately as a first step is pursuing peace.*

- Matthew 5:23–24 – "So if you are offering your gift at the altar and there remember that your brother has something against you, leave your gift there before the altar and go. First be reconciled to your brother, and then come and offer your gift."
  - *There is an intricate connection between our worship and our relational conflict. God cares so much about how we're living with one another that he instructs us to set the gift down, hit the pause button, and go make peace.*

For those who call on the name of Christ, we cannot claim ignorance, nor can we claim fatalism. Our Christianity is not some vaccine we take that protects us from being wronged, or even prevents us from wronging others. Instead, our Christianity gloriously provides a gospel answer for how we respond when unjust things happen.

Where the Rubber Meets the Road

This leaves us with a nagging question: *How am I really supposed to respond when my spouse sins against me?* Some people respond by insulting in turn. Some withdraw in silence, while still others get downright violent and vengeful.

How we react when wounded reveals quite a bit about us and our hearts. It reveals how much we think of our own rights and comfort, and how little we think of our own sin. Most fundamentally, it reveals how we think about God and the grace we've received. If we allow our hearts to drift from gratitude for our salvation, if we allow the joy we once had in Christ to become a distant memory, we run the risk of living a life that actively denies the salvation we so clearly profess.

How can we protect ourselves from the pitfalls that await every time we're offended or sinned against? Every married couple should accept three things.

1. *Offenses will happen.* Your spouse will inevitably sin against you or unintentionally offend you. And, you will inevitably sin against or unintentionally offend your spouse. Neither marital love nor marriage itself inoculates us from our sinful desires. You will sin against one another. The issue is not if, but when. Let's stop being surprised when it happens, and let's prepare for the inevitable.

2. *Offenses are never resolved by committing an additional offense.* This was modeled for us by the Savior himself: "When he was reviled, he did not revile in return; when he suffered, he did not threaten, but continued entrusting himself to him who judges justly" (1 Peter 2:23). My father would often say "Two wrongs don't make a right." Knowing that was true and that I had little wiggle room from conviction, I would regularly respond, "That's right, Dad. But one wrong and one right don't make a right either." Clever as that may be (and I thought it was pretty clever at the time), it is a response that is entirely Christless. When you accidentally cut yourself in your kitchen, your immediate response is to pull the knife away, put it down, and deal with the single wound. You don't respond by giving your hand a second slice. That's just common sense. As crazy as a "second slice" sounds, this is just what we do when we add another offense to our marriage. You and your

spouse are one flesh. If he or she injures the relationship, it makes no marital sense to add another cut. You want to move toward healing and treatment as quickly as possible.

3. *God is greater than the degree of offense.* Jesus entrusted himself to "him who judges justly" (1 Peter 2:23). He leaned upon the judgment and mercy and grace and love and long-suffering of God rather than whatever retribution or response he could offer himself.

With that in mind, our posture toward our spouse ought not to be one of defensiveness or shock in the face of their sin. It ought to be one of understanding and forgiveness. Yes, we will be offended from time to time. We will be sinned against. Our spouses are sinners, and sinners sin. Our posture should reflect this worldview and benefit from the greatness of our God of grace.*

We must go further still. In addition to understanding that our spouse is going to offend us (just as we will also offend them from time to time), our posture should be one of forgiveness that redirects our conversations. Not keeping a record of wrongs, but standing ready to release our spouse from the guilt of their sin and freeing them to enjoy grace instead, we respond in undeserved ways with unmerited grace.

How, then, can we develop an intentional reflex of forgiveness that redirects when sinned against? Entrust yourself to the one who judges justly and abide in him. The strength that

---

* Special wisdom and counsel is needed when dealing with abusive situations. Safety is paramount. If you find yourself in an abusive relationship, instead of applying this teaching, immediately seek safety and seek pastoral care. Allow someone to know what you're walking through so you can benefit from more specific help in your situation.

forgiveness requires can only come from Jesus, the One who forgives most greatly. The humility that grace requires can only come from the One who models perfect humility. A marriage characterized by forgiveness is one that is also characterized by joy, peace, and grace, to the glory of God.

So What Should We Do?

We sometimes deceive ourselves in relationships, don't we? We consider ourselves pretty evenhanded and kindhearted. When we act horribly or vengefully, we find escape and solace in the thought, *He (or she) made me do it.* We figure that the simple fact that we've been sinned against makes it okay to respond in kind. We assume such responses are understandable.

However, we know now those who first act against us do not control our reactions. It is possible to be wronged, even seriously persecuted, and bless in response (Romans 12:14). It is possible to be wronged without seeking to get even. We may ask how, but this is the whole point of the commands. We are not supposed to dig deeper into our own resources or bite our tongues harder to find the self-control. No, the type of living to which we're called is otherworldly. It is from the Spirit, not our flesh. It is gospel living.

So, let's say that a spouse sins against you in anger, or fails to remember something important. You don't have to be spiteful. You don't have to sin just because your spouse did. In fact, Christ-centered reactive living calls for quite the opposite. Our response is to be a blessing. *"He/She made me do it"* doesn't work in gospel living.

We must want more for our marriage than tit for tat. We must want more than the pettiness that the world produces, that we can find in any high school around the world. As adults, we should want more. As Christians we are called to more. And reading this book means you desire a better way forward.

In a blog focused on parental communication, my wife Gina eloquently captures this desire for redemptive communication.

> How I desire for my speech to distill as the dew, to refine and purify, rather than muddy [my children's] souls with harsh words and tones. I want to burn the picture in my brain of gentle rain falling on tender grass. A gentle rain that soaks and permeates the ground, refreshing and nourishing a parched, tender grass that can so easily be destroyed by harsh rains that rebound, run off, and damage.
>
> The tender souls of my children, souls we desperately want to fall at the foot of the cross, respond better to the gentle rain of Mom's pleasant countenance and grace-filled words and tones than to the driving, pounding, damaging stare or word that has nothing of Christ in it. Souls that need to hear recollections of what God has done, what he is doing, and what he will do. Living Water that sees beyond the busyness of the day to eternity and refreshes weary souls with grace for today and hope for tomorrow.[2]
>
> - Gina Flood

An eternal focus empowers you to respond to your husband or wife with mercy, kindness, humility, understanding, compassion, and patience. It acknowledges that the world neither rises nor falls on how each specific issue gets played out. In most cases, a comment made today can wait to be adjusted for another day or another moment. A forgotten loaf of bread from the shopping trip doesn't require a litany of other forgotten items on past trips; you can respond with patience. A dismissive tone from your spouse when you hoped for enthusiasm doesn't need a prosecutorial soliloquy, especially when you're angry or upset; you can respond with humility. A sarcastic quip of an answer doesn't require sarcasm in turn, especially if your spouse had a challenging day; you can respond in compassion.

Purposeful marital communication plays the long game. You're going to be spending the rest of your lives together. A time will come when emotions are not quite as charged, when the stakes are not quite as high. As husbands or wives, our focus is on the long haul. As Christians, our focus is eternal. We willingly embrace the reality that we all are being sanctified and will be ever changing, as we are ever in need of change.

Bottom Line

Now that you've read this chapter, you can be sure your spouse is going to say or do something that would otherwise provoke you. You have historically blamed the other person and felt like the pattern was unavoidable. You now know better. In his love, God will soon call you to practice this tool. Trust it, and trust him for it. You may just be amazed at the power demonstrated in the tool of first response.

Discussion/Reflection Questions

1. What thoughts come to mind as you consider Jesus as first responder? How should this truth impact your approach to communication?

2. How does the idea of grace inform your understanding of being a "first responder?" What role should that grace play in your marriage?

3. Three answers were suggested for the question, Why is this so hard for us? Which of those three seemed to hit closest to home?

4. Late in the chapter, the idea of an eternal focus was shared. In your own life, what provides the greatest challenge for keeping this focus?

5. What temptations do you believe might arise if you choose to be a good first responder while your spouse does not? How can you prepare now for that time?

Chapter 5

The Tool of Prayer

Anticipate your battles;
fight them on your knees before temptation comes,
and you will always have victory.[1]

- R. A. Torrey

And whatever you ask in prayer,
you will receive, if you have faith.

- Matthew 21:22

WE TEND TO eat a pretty healthy diet in our home, so it is not often that we have junk food, fried food, fun food. But when we do, we go all out. The Super Bowl is one of those annual occasions when we essentially throw all caution to the wind. On this momentous evening, the island in our kitchen is covered in appetizers that will make your mouth water, your belly ache, and your heart cry.

Because of her constant commitment to our family's nutritional health, my dear wife always puts out a veggie tray alongside the chicken fingers, spring rolls, and chips. Child after child goes to the island to fill their plates, never touching the veggie tray. As a faithful husband, after I fill my plate with the naughty food, I always take something from that tray just for posterity. Whether I eat it or not I can neither confirm nor deny.

For many of us, prayer in marriage is like the veggie tray at the Super Bowl party. You know it's good for you. You know avoiding it is bad for you. But it never occurs to us—at least not for long—that we should fill our plates first with the good stuff before we go to the other stuff. We should fill our marriages with prayer before all the rest.

One of the biggest reasons we think of prayer as the veggie tray is because we don't understand it. We don't often see it as one of the means by which we commune with God. We don't often see it as lovely and essential for life. In fairness, we are not going to be able to address the full subject of prayer in marriage. If that is a topic you'd like to study further, there are many good books out there.[2]

Our focus here is going to be narrowly aimed at prayer for and in marital communication. Some people skip reading about the topic of prayer because it makes them feel poorly, as though they are bad disciples. They are self-conscious because they deem their prayer life to be inadequate. This is not the goal of this chapter. The goal is to equip you with the tool of prayer so that your marriage can navigate the sometimes treacherous waters of communication, regardless of topic or setting.

Prayer as a Couple

Christians make a critical mistake when they segment their Christian life, artificially creating separation between things that should be linked. When you think through your day, there are some clear points of distinction. Your three meals are segmented properly: breakfast, lunch, and dinner. The day is helpfully segmented as well: morning, afternoon, and evening. These segments can help in planning a day. However, it is far less helpful to try to separate communication, sex, and prayer in your marriage.

You can have a successful lunch if you've failed at breakfast. Many times, your evening can still go perfectly well if you've had a rough morning. But marital sex will be significantly hindered if your communication is not doing well. In the same way, communication will suffer if your sex life is not healthy, and both will suffer if you're not praying. Far from separate segments, these items are intertwined like cords in a rope.

Prayer in marriage is not something you simply do before bed and meals. It is an ongoing lifestyle that should be part of every area of our lives. When understood as a communication tool, it does for your marriage what nothing else can.

Praying for Your Communication

When you and your spouse are communicating, there are many things going on at one time. There is the combination of words being spoken, body language, shared history, and individual desires and goals. If you've been married for long, you know this. But did you know that when you and your spouse are alone speaking with one another, there's another person present who has desires and goals as well?

When communication is thriving, there is a dynamic conversation occurring between three parties: the husband, the wife, and their God. The Spirit is at work *within* each spouse and *between* each spouse in the communication process. The unity of your marriage depends upon the ability to understand one another as you and your spouse seek to live as one flesh. The only way this can happen is with the help of God. And so, we should pray.

In Matthew 21:22, Jesus tells us, "And whatever you ask in prayer, you will receive, if you have faith." It is his joy to provide for us what we need for life and godliness. He delights to move in and through us in such a way that fosters unity and brings him glory.

So, with all of this power and help from God available to us, why is it that we still struggle with prayer in our marriage? Why do we not pray more? James gives us some insight. "You do not have, because you do not ask. You ask and do not receive, because you ask wrongly, to spend it on your passions" (James 4:2b–3). We either don't ask God for help or we ask for the wrong reasons.

Why Don't We Receive God's Help?

We don't ask.

There could be a million reasons why a couple would not ask God for help in their communication. Perhaps it simply does not occur to you because you've segmented your life. Perhaps you don't ask because you know you're sinning and you can't honestly ask God to help you sin. Perhaps you don't ask for help in marital communication because you don't pray at other times in your life. Perhaps you're slow to ask for help because you resist the reality that we all need help. Or perhaps your desires are so engaged in the stakes of a conversation that God isn't in the foreground of your thinking.

Go to God in all of these situations. He will answer. He is a good Father, giving good gifts to his children (Matthew 7:11). He wants to help you honor him. He wants to assist you in following his commands to love and respect one another. He wants you to be in unity as you parent your children together. He wants you to work through the many topics of marriage in a way that fosters trust and security. Our human efforts cannot generate this; only God can.

We ask for the wrong reasons.

When we pray, we are to pray in keeping with the will and Word of God. As a result, our prayers should be for things God could bless. It is right and proper to ask for the ability to share your thoughts with clarity. However, if you ask for clarity so you can shame or shut down your spouse on this issue, you should not expect God to help with that.

It is right and good to ask for your spouse to be receptive to what you're sharing. However, if the goal of your perspective is a sinful one, you should not expect God to make your spouse receptive. This is one of the ways prayer helps us in communication. At some point, our consciences wake up and we know we can't honestly pray for some things. If we do pause and pray, it has the effect of halting our sinful desires and resetting us to think as children of God.

Praying at All Times

Before you sit down for a conversation in your marriage, go to the Lord in prayer. If you are going to discuss a challenging topic, pray and ask for God's help to walk you through the challenges. If you are going to go out for the evening as a couple, ask God to empower you to keep your communication positive, helpful, and (most of the time, anyway) not focused on children.

Look carefully at the areas of communication that normally trip you up. Perhaps for your marriage that is any conversation about sex, money, schedules, or parenting. If you know you are going to talk about one of those topics, be purposeful to schedule that conversation. The "ambush" tactic doesn't often work for those topics. For example, if you schedule the conversation for a Sunday afternoon, you and your spouse can be praying about your upcoming interaction all week.

You can first pray *together* for that conversation. This frees you to come together as one before God prior to having the strain of the topic placed upon your relationship. You'll enter

Sunday afternoon stronger, more unified, and much more ready for the challenges.

In this way, we pray at all times for our communication because we need God's help at all times in our communication. I wish someone had shared earlier with me what the evangelist R. A. Torrey said on prayer. He said, "The reason why many fail in battle is because they wait until the hour of battle. The reason why others succeed is because they have gained their victory on their knees long before the battle came. ... Anticipate your battles; fight them on your knees before temptation comes, and you will always have victory."[3]

Anticipate the conversations and topics that may generate a battle, and talk with God about them before they occur. You will be surprised at the result.

Praying When It Gets Tough

Even when we pray, some conversations may drift toward conflict. You may be going along just fine when your spouse says something in the wrong way and, BANG, you feel like a grenade has gone off and it is wartime. Or maybe you've spilled your heart out and opened yourself up only to have your spouse underwhelm you with his or her care. You feel violated and want to avenge yourself. There's a better way.

In most sports, there is something akin to a time-out. In football, teams have three per half. In hockey, they have one per game. In baseball, time-outs take on the form of conversations or pitching changes. I'm never sure how many time-outs basketball teams have since they seem to be calling time out every twenty-five seconds. There are many reasons a team might call a time-out, but one reason is consistent across sports: managing momentum.

When the momentum is against you, sometimes you just need to stop the clock and regroup. If you're unfamiliar with this practice, you may be surprised how often it helps to stop the action. You gain your footing, get on the same page, and move forward with a plan.

Lest you think I'm encouraging you to take a time-out if your spouse starts getting momentum against you, let me remind you of something. Even though marital conflict seems like a spouse versus spouse situation, it most certainly is not. You and your spouse are on the same team. If one of you loses, you both lose. If you have a conversation that is straying from a godly direction, the enemy of your souls is the one gaining momentum. What should you do when this happens? Call a time-out. What might that actually look like? It looks like prayer.

That's right. In the middle of a brewing conflict, you do not need to continue with the momentum that is headed toward doom. You can stop right there and pray together. You can recognize before God that you've allowed the enemy to deceive you into being against each other rather than for one another. You can each ask God's forgiveness and plead for his help so that your spouse would be respected and your God glorified. Then you can start where you left off before you strayed.

How to Get Started

If you're unaccustomed to praying together, particularly in the midst of conflict, you may not know how to start. Where does a couple start when they are pitted against one another? You start by praying. I know that doesn't sound all that helpful, but let me illustrate.

Proverbs 4:7 has always struck my funny bone a bit. In making the case for us to get wisdom (not a laughing matter, to be sure), it says, "The beginning of wisdom is this: Get wisdom, and whatever you get, get insight."

It borders on sounding nonsensical: wisdom starts by getting wisdom. That is either super unhelpful or so revolutionary that it is mind-blowing to simple folk like me. I dare say it is the latter. The starting pistol in our race for wisdom bangs out a command: get wisdom. If we don't start by pursuing wisdom, we will never get wisdom. The same is true with prayer.

One of the greatest difficulties Gina and I faced with praying together was awkwardness. We were not used to praying together. The very thought of praying together was unappealing, and the discomfort paralyzed us, causing us discouragement each time we tried.

If that describes you, my suggestion is to pray. Just start praying. You will never figure out how to pray if you don't start. You will never grow comfortable praying together if you don't practice. Don't wait for your spouse to suggest it. If you're thinking about the need to pray, assume the Holy Spirit is prompting you to do so. The beginning of successful marital prayer is this: pray as a married couple. Just start praying.

Bottom Line

When you are about to begin a conversation with one another, pray as you open, earnestly inviting the third party in the room to participate. Prayer acknowledges God and asks for more than his help; it asks for his voice. Ask him to speak, and then listen. Passages of Scripture may come to mind. You may have a specific sense of what to pray for or an idea that wasn't there before. He knows what he's talking about, and he has your best interests in mind.

Discussion/Reflection Questions

1. How would you describe your personal prayer life? Is it a normal part of your walk with Christ, or is it something that is in need of much growth?

2. Are you in the habit of praying as a couple? Have you ever prayed as a couple? If so, what have you found that works for you? What doesn't work?

3. What obstacles do you face when you think of starting to pray? What fears come to your mind? Be specific and name them.

4. Are there couples who've been married longer than you that you could ask to pray for you? Consider inviting them to follow up with you and ask about your prayer time together as a couple.

5. Take a deep look at your communication patterns. When the time comes to pray, what do you or your spouse tend to do instead?

Chapter 6

The Tool of Physical Touch

Touch has a memory.[1]
- John Keats

But while he was still a long way off,
his father saw him and felt compassion, and ran
and embraced him and kissed him.
- Luke 15:20

THERE'S ONE IN every family or group of friends. You know, the one that is indescribably, intensely passionate about politics or exercise or clean eating. The evening is going just fine, then someone mentions "*the* topic" and everyone goes wide-eyed like you just said the name, *Voldemort*. All casual conversation and fun leave the room with a loud rushing sound, and the void is filled with awkward lobbying and poor persuasion.

Or perhaps it is a shared concern for a struggling friend or family member. While everyone is unified in their concern for this loved one, no one actually agrees on how to help them. Every time the name or the subject is mentioned, conflict breaks out. You can't really ignore the issue but everyone's impulse is to avoid it at all costs.

Everything seems fine if you just avoid *that* topic. You can be friends with this person, really good friends, if you just don't talk about it. And though the actual topic will vary from family to family, from group to group, the dynamic is the same.

Each of our marriages has the same type of challenges. Certain topics are just hazardous and divisive. You could be having a wonderful date with your spouse or a comfy evening side by side on the sofa, enjoying life, liberty, and the pursuit of happiness. And then out of nowhere *that* topic gets mentioned. Maybe the plot of the TV show you're watching is about money. Or the passage of Scripture you're reading together is about parenting. Or you need to have an important conversation with your parents, and you need to plan how it should go. You know what these topics are for your marriage. You already know one of those topics for us early in our marriage was communication.

Our relationships have the appearance of health until these "hot topics" come up. Then, when they pop up, all bets are off and the conversation or conflict or argument is filled with land mines, pitfalls, and snares. Sometimes it even starts going well and you both relax, only to find that the conversation takes a sharp turn downward. Wouldn't it great to know about that *before* it happened? Wouldn't it be great to keep a conversation on constructive tracks even if the topic is challenging?

This is where the tool of physical touch comes in. Just to be clear, I'm talking about touching that is purposely tender and purposely nonsexual. I'm talking about a connection that demonstrates you are for the other person and desiring to walk through this challenging topic in unity. I'm talking about affectionate touching. Have you ever noticed how hard it is to grow in anger toward someone whom you are touching affectionately? If not, you're in for a real treat and a great blessing to future conversations.

This tool serves husbands and wives in three different situations: when preparing for challenging conversations, when communication suddenly become tense, and when you are recovering from a failed attempt at healthy conversation. So, let's take these one at a time and examine this tool together.

Preparing for the Challenges

Preparing for challenging conversations is where the tool of physical touch is most useful. This is a difficult tool to apply after an argument has already begun. If you're communicating with raised voices and animated body language, you likely will want to swing back to the tool of prayer before continuing with this one. However, if you are about to enter a "hot topic zone" or even if you're concerned that tensions could rise, it is a perfect time for this tool.

During these types of conversations, it is best to sit down and pray together—and touch. In our marriage, we are usually at opposite ends of the couch with Gina's legs stretched out across mine while I hold them or we sit at a table holding hands. There's no magic or special blessing hanging in the balance on how you do this. The goal is just to be touching in a kind and tender way.

Most couples find it is difficult to fight with someone they are tenderly touching. You start in unity by touching, and then let the conversation progress. If it is going really well, you continue touching, perhaps even melting into one another as the concern for rising tensions dissipates. In these cases, beginning the conversation with touching has provided a physical reminder of the emotional and spiritual commitment you've made to be unified and on each other's side. The tool represents physically what you have hoped for relationally. But what if it is not going well? What then?

When We Stop Touching

Sometimes the tool does not work to prevent challenges. Perhaps you've plowed through the gentle obstacles that have been put in your way and tensions between you and your spouse are on the rise. This is where using the tool should kick into high gear.

You will find, often long before an actual argument breaks out, that you change the position of your body when you start becoming tense or angry. Agitation begins to set in, and you gradually withdraw from each other, separating hands or shifting so that her legs are no longer across yours. This is an involuntary physical cue that things are about to go downhill quickly.

When we stop affectionately touching our spouse, it is time to pause. Our conversation has begun to lose sight of its goal, and we are running off the tracks. Listen, there is no rule that says you have to continue running off the tracks. If your "hot topic" conversation has taken a detour through the land of conflict, every piece of wisdom says to stop right there. Remember, you will stop touching before the conflict breaks onto the scene. It's coming, to be sure, but it is not here yet. There's still time to remind one another that you are on each other's side.

Couples who struggle with conflict in communication often lose the battle right here. Each party knows things are starting to go poorly, but neither has the courage or knowledge to stop it. Physical touch helps you stay a step ahead of your conflict. You will see it or feel it before it really sets in. In that moment, when you realize you've stopped touching, you have a choice to make: stop fighting so you can keep on touching or stop touching so you can keep on fighting. You are no longer mainly face-to-face with your spouse; you are face-to-face with your pride.

Your pride is going to tell you in a hundred different ways that you are right and your spouse is wrong. Your pride will demand justice and a full hearing of your grievances. But your pride is not the one choosing the direction of the next few minutes of conversation—you are. Your pride will not be convicted of sin later in the evening—you will be. And your pride will not be the one needing to reconcile with your spouse— that's you again. Peace and unity in your marriage hang in the balance, and the choice for how you proceed is yours.

If you are going to benefit from the tool of physical touch, you're going to need to have a conversation with your pride before finishing the conversation with your spouse. You will need to tell your pride to get behind you so that you can walk in unity in the power of the Spirit. You will need to slay your pride as you humble yourself, acknowledging your contribution in allowing the conversation to get off track. And you may need to do this even if your spouse does not.

Then you take a step of faith. Ask your spouse if you can pick up the conversation where you were before you stopped touching. Ask if you can hold hands again (or whatever form of affectionate touching you were using). Pray together for God's help, and then continue your conversation. Or even take a break and pick up at another time, when the discussion might prove more fruitful.

Can you see that the tool still works even when things get a little tense? It flashes a warning sign you both need to remind you of your goal. It was the tether that kept you tied to one another. It was the very help you needed to navigate the "hot topic."

"But Rob," you may say, "we just had a blowup that created lots of damage. Can this tool help a couple like us?"

Touching in the Aftermath

There are likely going to be times when you blow it. When the godly goals you've set your eyes on become obscured and you say and do things you never thought you'd say or do. We've all been there. You're not alone in your communication failures or in your regret for your words or actions.

It is so hard to come together and show affection in the aftermath of a sinful conflict. It is hard to hug or hold hands or gently kiss one another goodnight. You may share a bed that evening, but the space between you seems like a mile even though you're in the same bed. Physically touching seems impossible.

I don't recommend that you begin to reconcile through this tool. It is likely too soon. You will first need to apply other tools from this middle section as well as the closing two chapters of the book. How will you know you've been reconciled and the unity of your relationship has been restored? It is often not in the moment one spouse extends forgiveness. That may be the most important part, but it is not the clearest way to know. You'll know when you can affectionately touch again.

In the aftermath of communication failures, physical touch is not the first tool for reconciliation. It is the tool that reveals reconciliation has taken place. Don't rush this. If you rush affectionate touching in the aftermath of a conflict you run the risk of deepening the damage. This is exponentially worse when you rush sexual touch. Trust God. Be patient. Be humble. Exercise compassion and discipline in your relationship. Don't rush physical touch, but do pray for it.

Ask permission from your spouse before going there. "Can I hold your hand?" "Would you allow me to hug you?" This may feel weird, but it ensures that physical touch is entirely mutually desired. If he or she says no or asks for more time, grant it. Remember, being patient not only honors your spouse's wishes, it honors God. When your spouse is ready, thank God for it. Don't take affectionate touch for granted. But remember to use physical touch at the beginning of the "hot topic" conversations because it is much easier to prevent the conflict than it is to recover from it.

Bottom Line

I recently rented a vehicle while on a ministry trip. I was driving down the highway and suddenly heard beeping and a strangely shaped light appeared on my dashboard. Then it went away. After this cycle occurred a few times, I determined to figure out what it was. (It is important for you to know that I drive old cars that don't do fancy things like this. When my car beeps, my engine is about to blow.)

This rental car had a "lane departure warning system." It was warning me when it thought I was getting too close to the lines that separate the lanes. If I drifted toward one, the car yelled at me. If I went back to the center of my lane, it stopped beeping. If I had my turn signal on, it knew I wanted to cross the lines, so it did not beep.

The tool of physical touch does this for your marriage. It won't stop you from driving off the road, but it will alert you when it looks like that's where you're headed. It is the beep that says "Get back into the center of the lane." Listen to it. It is there to help you. Treasure it as you seek to treasure one another.

Discussion/Reflection Questions

1. What are the topics in your marriage that might be best served by the tool of physical touch? Compare answers with your spouse for this question.

2. How does your marriage do with nonsexual touch? Are you a couple who affectionately touches often? Do you rarely touch? Think and talk through these dynamics.

3. In what way would you prefer to be touched when talking about difficult topics? Think through your preferences and share them with your spouse.

4. Have you ever been helped by a well-timed, well-intentioned, appropriate touch? A hug? A squeeze of the hand? Share that experience and how it helped you.

Chapter 7

The Tool of Mirroring

How much better to get wisdom than gold!
To get understanding is to be chosen rather than silver.
- Proverbs 16:16

An intelligent heart acquires knowledge,
and the ear of the wise seeks knowledge.
- Proverbs 18:15

AMERICAN TELEVISION HAS a long history of sitcoms. The formula for the sitcom, regardless of which one we're talking about, is to set up a scenario that resonates with where the audience lives, and then take it one step further to the ludicrous. One of the tools sitcoms use often is misunderstanding.

A teen is invited to go with a friend's family to Rome. Thrilled for the opportunity, she eventually realizes they're not going to Rome, Italy, but to Rome, Wisconsin. A husband is seen with another woman and presumed by friends to be unfaithful. Confused when they confront him, it becomes clear the woman is a Realtor working with the couple to buy a house. The situations are endless, but they all have misunderstanding, confusion, and wrong assumptions at the heart of the story.

What is needed is something that introduces clarity to the situation, something that uncovers the incorrect assumptions and brings greater understanding and, therefore, less conflict to the relationship. Granted, it would make lousy TV, but it could make much healthier relationships. When we labor through communication failures in marriage, there's no audience laughing and enjoying the confusion. There's just a husband and a wife who have no idea why they're arguing, except that they feel the other does not understand them.

Enter the tool of mirroring. Mirroring means one person repeats in their own words what they understand the other to be saying. It can help couples avoid unnecessary conflict and deliver them from the significant ramifications of misunderstanding.

The Basis for the Tool

There are many passages of Scripture that encourage the Christian to seek understanding—to draw out the intentions of the heart, the deep waters within a man. Proverbs 22:17 sums up the various commands and exhortations, "Incline your ear, and hear the words of the wise, and apply your heart to my knowledge."

Whenever two people are in conversation, they depend upon words to carry the intentions of their minds and hearts. Words are the means God has given us for communication. As powerful as words are, they are not always up to the task of perfectly conveying our intentions. We must not only find wise and healthy ways to articulate our thoughts, but our thoughts must also be rightly interpreted and understood.

Have you ever said something you thought was clear, but the person you were talking to heard something else? You want to stop the conversation and insist that you're being misunderstood. The interpretation is not what you meant. But as soon as you try to clarify, you come across as either attacking your listener or being defensive.

Conversely, have you ever been certain of what your spouse meant with his or her words, but they disagree with your interpretation? You read the tone of voice, body language, and the context of the situation, and you came to a clear understanding of what was communicated. The only problem is that he or she insists your interpretation is inaccurate.

Misunderstandings like this can make for very frustrating communication. Confusion and irritation set in, and we don't press on to achieve understanding or unity. You're left wondering what she meant by this sharp comment or what he was hoping for with that tone of voice. And in most cases, you just give up on communication, settled in your misjudgments, and divided within your own home.

As Gina and I recovered from the rocky start of our marriage, we needed to rebuild understanding and truth. We learned early on that we couldn't presume that our initial understanding was correct. We needed to check and verify. We needed to clarify. We learned to mirror one another's statements to be sure that the communication one of us intended was what the other received.

What would happen if we all leaned toward gaining understanding and away from elevating our own understanding? Proverbs 3:5 already calls us to be suspect of our own understanding. What if we just left open the possibility that our initial take on the intentions in our spouse's heart might be incorrect? What if we tested it with an approach of humility and understanding? What if we used the tool of mirroring?

The Use of the Tool

With any number of words, phrases, or techniques, the point is to summarize in your own words what you hear your spouse saying. It will help you test whether you are hearing your spouse properly. Once your spouse makes a point, repeat it back to them. Say something like "So, what I hear you saying is …" or, "Are you saying …?"

I want to emphasize the "question" part of the tool. You are not declaring back to them with ironclad certainty what they mean. You are explaining what you understand them to mean, and then you are asking if you are correct. Now comes the pivotal part of this exercise. Ready? You must allow your spouse either to affirm or to correct what you've said. If they say you got it wrong, you don't get to say "No I didn't." You simply reply, "Ok, can you try explaining what you're saying again, please?" They get the final say defining what they mean. Paul provides plain instruction here for us when he says "Love… believes all things" (1 Corinthians 13:7b). This is how to use this tool with fairness and in good faith. Not only is this right, but it is what *you* would want if the roles were reversed.

Both spouses share the power of the tool of mirroring. The spouse who "mirrors" presses toward understanding. He or she values loving, respectful comprehension so highly that the conversation cannot progress until this type of understanding is reached. This is a powerful demonstration of relational unity that honors the dignity of both husband and wife.

Humility and a commitment to integrity before God are necessary ingredients for this tool to be effective. A genuine heart for the good of your spouse is critical. Without those ingredients, the conversation is bound to fall apart or be used to manipulate and control. But *with* those ingredients, you'll find you stop missing one another. You'll stop running circles or taking an hour to have a ten-minute conversation. You'll find that you actually communicate.

The Challenge of the Tool

At first, applying this tool might feel quite awkward and clumsy, which makes it challenging to get started. I remember a time about fifteen years ago when my golf swing was analyzed by a video program. They had four or five different cameras on me as I drove a golf ball. I then hit a fairway iron followed by a wedge. After about five balls, I waited for the analysis.

Apparently, at that point in perfecting my game, I had what was called a "chicken wing" swing. For you nongolfers, this is not a good thing. In short, my right elbow was not where it ought to have been. It was flapping in the wind, I suppose. As part of the package, an instructor came and showed me how to remedy the problem. I hit an entire bucket of balls with my right wing tucked in and hated every minute of it. I'm sure it was more correct, but it felt awful and even hurt a bit. Discouraged and not believing it was worth the challenge, I embraced my chicken wing swing and kept shooting in the nineties. For you nongolfers, this is not a good thing either.

This is what it can feel like to practice mirroring. At first, you're likely to find that repeating each other in an already challenging conversation feels laborious and a bit silly. You're going to want to revert to more natural ways of communicating. Under the weight of the awkwardness, you're going to forget that your more innate ways of communicating are the ones that got you into the mess to begin with. You're going to want to quit.

Let me encourage you—press on. All new things feel awkward. Even new shoes need to be broken in. Unity in your marriage is worth the awkwardness. Achieving understanding is worth the extra time. And having a husband or wife who knows he or she is being heard, loved, and understood is worth whatever it takes.

You'll find that in time mirroring will flow much more naturally for you. You may even discover, after much practice, that it is no longer necessary. This is the goal of all of the tools: to help you more skillfully and successfully communicate with your spouse for the health of your marriage to the glory of God.

The Surprising Result of the Tool

When Gina and I started using this tool, I made a surprising discovery. It turns out that I didn't like Gina's summaries of my statements. She would summarize my words in good faith, but they always came back to me with an edge to them. She seemed consistently uncharitable and negative in her summaries. So I naturally did not affirm her mirroring and tried to explain myself differently. Essentially, her summaries would remain the same.

In time, I learned that her summaries were actually quite accurate. When I was speaking, I was the one with the edge, with the undertones and overtones. She was picking them up loud and clear, but because you couldn't trace them on a transcript of the conversation, I had reasonable doubt on my side. Mirroring did more than help Gina understand the intentions behind my words. It helped me understand my own intentions when I heard them come out of her mouth.

Bottom Line

The point of mirroring is to reveal how you both are being heard and seen. As you listen to your spouse echo back to you what you're saying and how you're saying it, you begin to see in the foreground what you prefer to keep in the background—your motivations. You are no longer seeking to be right. You are seeking unity and understanding between you and your spouse. You are seeking clarity on how you may be acting in unbelief or out of fear. When the tool is used properly, you are also seeking to hear your spouse accurately. If you seek to understand rather than defend your own assumptions, then you are primed for success through the tool of mirroring.

Discussion/Reflection Questions

1. Have you ever been in a conflict that began because you were misunderstood? What feelings did you experience? What frustrations did you face? What do you wish your spouse had done to better understand you?

2. What are some things that get in the way of proper understanding? Think of motives, emotions, or even circumstances.

3. Why do you think it is essential to allow the one speaking to define what they mean? What are the benefits of holding to this principle? What dangers might there be if you avoid that principle?

4. In what ways can mirroring help a relationship through a difficult conversation?

5. How can you prepare for the awkward stages of using this tool? Think through the challenges you and your spouse may face and make a plan to address them.

Chapter 8

The Tool of Proper Timing

For everything there is a season,
and a time for every matter under heaven.
- Ecclesiastes 3:1

A person finds joy in giving an apt reply—
and how good is a timely word!
- Proverbs 15:23 (NIV)

EARLY IN MY adulthood, I worked in the music field. With a degree in music, I spent nearly the first decade of my professional life teaching music and conducting. In music, timing is everything. One of the first things you'll see on any piece of music is the tempo—how quickly or slowly the song should be played. If the drums are playing at one speed and the guitar at a different speed, you have chaos; harmonies are destroyed. Even if all of the notes are played correctly, the music is wrong if the timing is wrong.

One of the great functions of a conductor is to set and keep the tempo. Every musician in the orchestra keeps an eye on the conductor so that he or she can keep in step with the others. Every songwriter or composer will tell you that notes are created to occur in moments, and skillful musicians know how to bring those notes and moments together.

When they are played in those moments, the notes are wonderful. When they miss their moments, the notes create a cacophony.

Enter the tool of proper timing. The principle here is simple: *words* are intended for *moments*, and the skillful communicator learns how to bring words and moments together. You may recall we spent some time in chapter 1 covering this from Ephesians 4. (See principle 3 in chapter 1.)

Many of us are very good at this skill in our lives broadly. If you need to ask for a raise at work, you are not simply going to let that spill out of your mouth at the water cooler or in the parking lot. You look for just the right time, when your boss is in just the right mood. And you ask in the most respectful way with carefully chosen words. This is not manipulation, or at least it doesn't have to be. It can simply be wisdom.

Or think about a friend who is making destructive choices. You want your help to be received well so you don't just drop your concerns on them via text message. You wait for a time when you're face-to-face and have time to discuss the issue at length. You may even pray for God to help you use the right words and give you appropriate timing.

The frustrating part of proper timing is how well we do this in the rest of life and how poorly we seem to apply it in our marriages. We understand the sensitive nature of words and timing in our work relationships, in our friendships, in our church relationships, and with our neighbors. But somehow we think of our spouse as something less than the three-dimensional humans those other people are. It doesn't have to be that way. We can do better, and we must.

The Everyday Ebb and Flow

While every home and every marriage is unique, there are common elements to all marriages. When you are doing life together, there is a rhythm, a normal routine that settles in. The routine becomes so common and so familiar that we actually don't often notice it at all. I'm asking you to notice it. Study it. Learn what your ebb and flow is as a couple. And then use it for good. Here are a few things to consider.

Times of chaos

Typically, the first opportunity Gina and I have to talk about the day is when I arrive home from work. We often take time then to catch up on the events of the day, but this is not the time for careful conversation on sensitive or even important topics. We have children running around needing rides to this or that while dinner gets put on the table and homework gets completed. Although it is important for me to know what has transpired with my family, it is not the time to work out any challenges or disagreements.

If something recently occurred that Gina and I must discuss at length, we will wait until after dinner when the younger children are asleep and the older children are otherwise engaged. To bring up an important topic at any other time is to invite frustration and ineffectiveness. We cannot avoid all conversation as we wait for the chaos to dissipate. There is always activity in our home with people going in or out. We must talk amidst the din of the family. But we also must be purposeful. Some things ought not to be discussed with the children around simply because the topics are not appropriate for them to hear. Or perhaps we need to have more than three uninterrupted minutes for a fruitful conversation.

Don't hate the chaos. It is part of the great blessing of family. But don't ignore it either. Learn the chaotic times, navigate them, and choose wisely what you attempt to accomplish during them.

Times of fatigue

I took a long time early in our marriage to learn how to manage daily fatigue. I still struggle from time to time. Somewhere around 10 p.m. I hit my stride for mental clarity. I've always been an evening person. It's not that I intend to talk about serious things late at night; it's just that they occur to me late at night.

As God has designed it, I have married a morning person. She'd be open to having a 6 a.m. sit-down conversation, but a serious conversation at 10 p.m. is not going to catch her at her best. You can imagine her frustration when we put our heads on our pillows and I ask to talk about the children or our intimate life. She'd love to have those conversations and is blessed when I bring them up—just not at bedtime.

Within the normal flow of life, there are good times and bad times, even for good conversations. Learn the ebb and flow of your marriage. More importantly, learn your spouse's ebb and flow. And then apply what you learn to the conversations you have.

Times of charged emotion

There is a relationship between our emotions and our ability to hear. It is what they call an inverse proportion. The higher your emotions, the lower your ability to hear. What is even trickier is that your elevated emotions can be about something entirely separate from the topic on the table, but the inverse proportion still exists. Let me explain.

Imagine that I want to talk with Gina about something when I get home from work. I want to plan a different kind of family vacation this year, which will be a bit of a departure from previous years. I've got my pitch ready and my questions for her. I get home and find that she has had a very challenging day. Our oven has broken, leaving dinner only half baked, and one of our children has accidentally spilled a drink into our computer keyboard. One of the other children has failed to do the assigned chores, and because of the compounding chaos, Gina didn't have time to exercise today.

She's managing the frustration and seeking to find God in the midst of it. Let me ask you, would this be the proper time to talk about altering our vacation plans this summer? Will she even be able to hear the nuanced pitch I've created? The answers are no and no. And this is not her fault. It is a time of charged emotion, and it is incumbent upon me to know this.

There are many times for each of us that the emotion of the day calls for the other to delay an important conversation. It is love expressed in a practical way. We extend this kind of compassion and deference to others on a regular basis. We must master the skill of extending the same courtesy to our spouse.

Times of vulnerability

I want to hit one more item in the everyday ebb and flow times of vulnerability. You may be in one of those purposeful, well-timed, deep conversations when one of you opens up and shares an unguarded part of your heart. This is a holy moment in marriage. It is also a moment that must be treated tenderly and wisely. Perhaps you've prayed over all you hope to say in this conversation and things seem to be going well. But you did not anticipate her laying her heart bare like this. You did not foresee him opening his soul.

It's time to reexamine your script. Are your goals still appropriate or should you defer because of how vulnerable your spouse is? Has God seen fit to accomplish something unplanned in this conversation? Can you release the details to his loving care and nurture your spouse in this moment?

It is possible to stick to your agenda and say something that is accurate—even biblical—and still create deep hurt and relational division. Don't miss the holiness of that moment. And don't be rough with it. Words are intended for moments. Is this the right moment for those words?

There's Nothing Wrong with a Schedule

With any number of dynamics flowing through everyday life, you may wonder how you're supposed to cover all you must cover in marital conversation if you're being so careful about timing. In reality, very few things demand to be discussed right here and now. Almost everything can wait an hour or a day or even more. I've shared with many couples that there's nothing wrong with creating a schedule.

I remember a time in my life when I did not keep a calendar. My life was simple enough, and my brain was uncluttered. I could remember things because I was sharper, less was demanded of me, and I had fewer commitments. Now, without a calendar, I can sometimes forget to eat.

At work, calendars keep things moving. I have weekly meetings with my administrative assistant at church to be sure we are functioning on the same page with appointments, projects, and events. I meet with the office staff at the same time every month to be sure we're functioning as a team and all headed toward the same goal. We have members meetings throughout the church calendar to be sure we're communicating with the congregation regularly. These practices are not unique to my church. These are just healthy team patterns that foster success and unity.

When have you scheduled your weekly meeting to be sure you and your spouse are on the same page? Maybe you have—good for you. You're off to a great start. Maybe you've known you needed a weekly meeting but never took the step to finalize it. You're halfway there. Maybe you never thought of scheduling a meeting with your spouse and still think it's a silly idea. Let me help you with that.

Couples who don't plan to communicate are not going to communicate well. Without a time to sit down and discuss things like finances, parenting, and house maintenance, you are left to bring subjects up while guessing at the proper timing. You won't be postured for physical touch since you'll be talking while doing other things. You won't have the calmness or time for mirroring. Limiting your marriage to spontaneous conversation works just fine—until it doesn't.

If you have something you want to discuss with your spouse, how much easier is it to simply add it to the list for Wednesday's conversation? You don't have to wonder when you'll get to it. You can plan to keep that evening free on those days. You can even plan meals that require only simple prep and clean up. The kids can know Wednesdays are reading nights for *them* so mom and dad can talk *to one another.*

If you're not in the habit of doing this, try it for three to six months and be faithful to protect and use the time. You'll be surprised at how it simplifies things.

When It Just Can't Wait

What do you do when you just can't delay a conversation? When a conversation is critical to have at that very moment, you talk. Bedtime gets delayed or the kids get dismissed.

And you rush to employ the other tools. You pray. You refuse to take offense by responding in a way that fosters peace. You mirror back and forth to ensure you understand one another. You find a way to touch affectionately so that you're monitoring how your relationship is doing in the midst of this urgent conversation.

The timing can't be perfect for every conversation. As long as this is not the norm for you and is the exception rather than the rule, you will have built a lot of trust with your spouse and can count on God to provide the grace you need to meet you and your spouse in those important, more urgent situations.

Bottom Line

Most of us understand this tool and apply it generously in our other circles of influence. We are savvy and wise in how and when we talk elsewhere. Let's commit to making our marriage a relationship filled with our greatest wisdom and most careful communication. Let's apply this tool of thoughtful timing (and the rest of the tools) in such a way that prioritizes our marriage as the most important earthly relationship we have. And let's strive before God for communication that honors him and brings him glory.

Discussion/Reflection Questions

1. In what ways do you practice the tool of proper timing in your life? Consider work, time with extended family, friends, etc. How have you seen this aid your communication?

2. What is your preferred time of day for challenging conversations? When do you feel you are at your best to handle those topics? Share you answer with your spouse and have your spouse share with you. Seek to arrive at a workable and agreed-upon time moving forward.

3. Which of the four categories listed under the title "The Everyday Ebb and Flow" provides the greatest challenge for you? For your spouse? Describe and explain.

4. When might you plan a purposeful time for communicating? Pick a day and time that works for both of you. What might stand in the way of doing so?

5. What are some scenarios that could arise where you will have to waive the proper timing? As you make your list, try to keep it very short.

Section 3:

Working It Out

NOW THAT YOU have some tools for more effective, Christ-honoring communication with your spouse, all that is left is practice. If you've ever tried to become proficient at something, you know there is an Achilles heel to the process: discouragement. You must not try these tools once or twice and declare them a failure. To truly be helpful to your marriage, the tools must be applied repeatedly.

I have always been fascinated by the piano. When I was seventeen, I asked my father if he'd help me buy a keyboard. He was puzzled since I did not play piano nor had I ever had lessons. I just thought I could figure it out if I had one. Eventually I persuaded him to make the purchase. (As a father of grown and growing children, only now do I have an understanding of how crazy I sounded.)

After my first night of playing on my new keyboard, I thought I had made an awful decision. I was no better three hours later than I was when I started. What had I done!? Well, I can tell you what I hadn't done; I hadn't practiced enough. By God's grace, after countless hours on that keyboard (and many other pianos throughout the years), I was proficient enough to major in music and make it my career prior to pastoring. But oh, did I require practice!

I'm sure you care more about your marriage than I did about my keyboard—at least I hope you do! In our pursuit of better communication for stronger marriages, let's be in the business of pressing on, staying in the game, and refusing to quit. It is my hope this section helps you continue this good work and grow in and through the grace of God.

Discussion/Reflection Questions

Preparing for Section Three

1. Once a marital conflict is over, how quickly do you and your spouse reconcile? How long does it take for the relationship to feel restored?

2. How well do you do at setting your spouse's wrongdoing behind you? Do you find yourself keeping a record of wrongs and harboring bitterness?

3. Time to check in on how your hope is doing. As you look at the communication challenges you face in your marriage, do you have hope for growth? Rate it on a scale from 1 to 10.

Chapter 9

The Tools on Display

*Let's discipline ourselves
so that our words are few and full.
Let's become known as people who
have something to say when we speak.*[1]
- Richard Foster

God opposes the proud, but gives grace to the humble.
- James 4:6

SOLUTIONS IN MARRIAGE are not "one size fits all." While biblical instruction and biblical wisdom are intended for all people, what that looks like in the nitty-gritty of life will vary widely from one couple to another, from one home to another, from one church to another, from one culture to another, and from one era to another.

Harken back to the opening chapters when we met the Joneses, the Wilsons, and the Butlers. Each couple struggled with different challenges. They each came from different backgrounds and were married for different periods of time. Will growth look the same for each couple? Of course not.

We must be careful not to assume that what works for the Floods will work the same for the Butlers. We must be careful whenever we seek to compare the Wilsons with the Joneses.

We must embrace the reality that working out our challenges, working with these tools, will require one application for their marriages and another application for our marriage.

To illustrate this point, let's take a close look at these three couples walking through the same situation. We'll explore their various responses, their application of different tools, and we will confront the lie that our circumstances control our responses. Read on to see which elements of each couple's responses map onto your marriage and circumstance. Then apply what you can and adjust what must be adjusted.

The Scenario[2]

Several times per year, First Community Church holds marriage events for all couples in the church. At each meeting, the married couples gather for a message from the pastor followed by discussion and fellowship. This evening they're launching a series based on this book, *With These Words: Five Communication Tools for Marriage and Life.* The first lesson is based on Ephesians 4:29 and highlights the importance of using words to build up, knowing the need of the moment, and giving grace with our words. (See chapter 1 for a review).

The goal for the evening is to equip married couples to honor God in their communication. Much of the pastor's counseling load reveals a weakness in this area and the hope—the prayer—is that this corporate teaching can help many marriages all at once. As planned, the sixty or so couples in attendance meet in small groups after the message to discuss the material. The meeting ends in a brief time of prayer. Then the pastor locks up the church and heads home, as do those in attendance. The night's work is over for him, but the excitement has just begun for some of the couples.

Checking in on "Yeah, Let's Talk...Oh Wait, Not about That" (from Chapter One)

You'll recall Tom and Marcy Butler are new to First Community and seem to have a great marriage—at least it's great so long as they avoid talking about intimacy. Neither of them knows how to talk about it so they avoid the subject. This doesn't help their intimacy, and it certainly doesn't help their communication.

They both enjoyed the message and were in full agreement with one another. Yet, one of the discussion questions shared in their group gave them each a pit in their stomach: *Is there a topic you need to discuss, but avoid because of fear? What is it and why?* Naturally, they didn't share their situation in the group, but they both felt like God had been reading their mail and they were afraid to be alone after the meeting. On the ride home, neither of them mentioned anything.

It wasn't until they were shutting down the house before bed that Tom said, "Hey Marcy, do you think we should talk about what happened tonight?" Even though many things had happened that night, she knew exactly what Tom was referring to. "I don't know, Tom. I mean, yes, I suppose we should talk about it, but should we do that now? What did you think of Pastor's opening illustration? It was funny, wasn't it?"

How can the tools help a couple like the Butlers? The tool of physical touch will go a long way in assuring each of them of the safety of the situation, or at least indicating to them when the helpfulness of the conversation is waning. The tool of proper timing is critical so they have this conversation when they're at their best. When they finally share, the tool of mirroring will serve them to be sure there is no misunderstanding or blame shifting. The tool of first response can help them know how best to reply when a single comment is made that might be challenging to hear or one that is spoken with imprecision. And the tool of prayer is not only the best way to start and finish this conversation, but it stands in the wings ready to swing in and help if the conversation gets too challenging.

The Butlers are a solid couple who genuinely desire to nurture a God-honoring relationship. But they are not entirely healthy. Utilizing the five communication tools will help the Butlers grow, even when the topic is hard.

Of course, the Butlers weren't the only couple at the meeting. The Wilsons and the Joneses were there too. Let's visit with the Wilsons.

Revisiting "All Quiet on the Domestic Front" (from Chapter Two)

You may recall Darryl and Linda Wilson's parallel lives. With the kids out of the house, they spend most of their days avoiding conflict and avoiding each other. They don't often attend these couples' meetings, but their small group leader rallied their members to sit together, which would have made their absence quite noticeable.

As they listened to the pastor teach from Ephesians 4:29, they wondered what he was talking about. *Words that give grace and encourage, words that build up*—these were foreign concepts to them. Most of Darryl's words focused on the bills, the yard, and his retirement. Most of Linda's words focused on the weather, the grandkids, and the health of their aging parents.

When the message was done, they were blown away that other couples were willing to share openly in the discussion groups. Though it seemed like the group leader wanted them to share, neither of them said a word during the entire discussion time. Quietly in Linda's heart, she wondered what might happen if they tried to talk about something of substance. She saw other couples who could do that and desired it. Meanwhile Darryl heard one of the men share his purposefulness in having marital conversation and felt convicted.

They got in their car to drive home, each wanting a bit of what they saw, but neither having any idea how to get there. The five-minute ride home was silent, making it feel like fifty. The tension was so thick you could cut it with a knife. Darryl eventually reached over to turn on the radio. They sat quietly, listening to music the entire way home. Darryl made his way to the TV, and Linda made her way to the bedroom. They went to sleep and awoke to the same routine that had marked their lives for thirty-seven years. With a sorrow-filled awkwardness, all is still quiet on the domestic front.

Let's apply the tools for the Wilsons to see how they can move toward healthier communication. The tool of prayer is a great place to start. It is likely that neither Darryl nor Linda thinks the other is very safe to try something new with. In cases like that, it can be so helpful for Darryl and Linda to go to the One who is in fact safe for them and ask for his help.

They are almost certainly not proficient in articulating their thoughts and feelings—not with one another anyway. Using the tool of touch, they can in faith hold hands and share. Then, to be sure they remain in step with one another, they could use the tool of mirroring, carefully repeating what the other is saying. For instance, "Alright, Darryl, I hear you saying _____. Is that what you're saying?" "Linda, am I hearing you right when you say _____?"

Either of them could circle back around to the content of the conference and suggest taking just one of the discussion questions from the group and talking it through. "Hey Linda," Darryl could begin. "What do you think if we sit down and go back to those questions the pastor gave us the other night? I've thought about it, and I would like to share some things God showed me." Following that significant step, they could stop and thank God in prayer, leaving the rest of the questions for subsequent Sundays. The Wilsons need to take small steps of obedience, moving toward each other. With these steps, there's hope for God to be glorified through their communication. The five tools will give the Wilsons practical ways for starting to build healthy patterns of communication into their marriage.

Next let's peek in on the Joneses and see how the evening went for them.

Returning to "The War of the Joneses" (from Chapter Three)

You may recall Bill and Shirley's on-again/off-again relationship prior to their wedding. You may also recall their explosive arguments that lead only to hurt and division. When they heard that the meetings at First Community Church were going to focus on communication, they each separately felt a degree of hope. Even though these types of meetings normally kick off more conflict, they hope that maybe this time the teaching will help. Maybe they'll get some insight or pointers or some miracle from God. It's hard for them to imagine the remainder of their lives being spent fighting as they do.

As they listened to the message, Bill thought the pastor nailed it on the head. He was making wonderful points, and the application was easy to understand. In all honesty, though, the foremost thought in his mind was, *I sure hope Shirley is getting this. She seems to be paying attention, so maybe things will change for the better this time.*

Shirley thought the pastor nailed it too. She always appreciates the teaching at First Community, and tonight was no different. She was taking notes vigorously as she looked over at

Bill. He was just sitting there with a serious expression on his face. She couldn't really tell if he was listening closely or not. His Bible wasn't open and his notebook was on the floor under his chair. She thought she might even have seen him nod off. Knowing she couldn't allow this opportunity to pass, Shirley stopped taking notes for herself and started taking notes for Bill. If he didn't love God or her enough to listen carefully, she would love God enough to listen for him.

During the first small group discussion question, they knew there were going to be problems that evening. "What was one point that stood out to you from the message?" Each of them subtly implied a change that was needed in the other person, not in themselves. They kept it together in their discussion group, but the ride home was a different story.

They hadn't left the parking lot before Shirley asked Bill if he was even listening to the message. Bill couldn't tolerate Shirley's snarky tone. His retort set the course for the remainder of the evening: "You know what, how about you just tell me what you think Jesus wants me to do so I can give you the list I made for YOU!?"

"Don't make this about me. At least I was taking notes!" was her bitter comeback. He paused in disbelief. "Unbelievable! You took notes for me *again*?!" The war of the Joneses was raging once again.

Having learned about the tools, let's sit in the back seat of their car. As Shirley jabbed with her snarky comment, what options were available to Bill? With the tool of first response, he could have replied with an honest and uncharged question: "I sure was listening. I thought the pastor did a great job. Did it seem like I wasn't listening?" Even if Shirley's response continued to be critical—"Well, you didn't even take notes!"—he could calmly articulate some of the mental notes he made from the sermon. This would have demonstrated that he was listening, calming Shirley's fears of a disengaged husband. The conversation could then have been redirected toward discussing the content of the sermon, rather than fighting over Shirley's judgmental attitude.

Shirley could have started the conversation quite differently, referring to one of the points from the message itself (Ephesians 4:29), and chosen to speak words of grace as her first volley. "The pastor did a great job, didn't he? Where do you think we're already doing well?" Even if she was choking back her judgment with every syllable, her words could have given grace and provided a more constructive path for the evening. Either of them could have paused after a jab from the other, recognizing the devolving nature of their conversation, and asked if they could pray.

In the war of the Joneses, both Mr. and Mrs. Jones had God's power. He would have helped turn their communication from destructive to constructive, from ungodly to godly, from tearing down to building up. Neither was powerless, and therefore neither can place the ultimate blame for the awful evening on the other. Utilizing the five communication tools could have brought them closer to a place of unity and reminded them that they were on the same team.

Tying It All Together

The pages and stories from this chapter could go on and on and on. There is no end to the situations where healthy communication is needed in marriage. There is no end to the eccentricities and specific details that make each marriage unique. No one book or one sermon or one article can summarily address every marital situation. But there are principles, both biblical and wisdom, which can guide us no matter the situations we face.

While the Joneses, Wilsons, and Butlers are fictional couples, their stories represent real scenarios where communication tools could help. More than the tools, the Scriptures we covered equip us with Christlike love and motivation that give us courage and patience that are not naturally ours. We then take that courage and remember that apart from Christ we can do nothing. We press toward the brokenness, no matter how broken it feels, and we entrust our marriages to God.

As you work through these tools, you are going to discover you need more than a biblical understanding of words. You are going to need more than a set of helpful communication tools. You are going to need the Spirit to move in and through you so that the relationship continues to function and grow as you get good at communication. The next two chapters are designed to help you progress from knowledge to the experience of forgiveness, grace, and mercy.

Discussion/Reflection Questions

1. As you think through the couples in this chapter, is there one that seems most like your marriage relationship? In what ways are you similar? In what ways are you different?

2. Is there an application of the tools that seems most relevant to your current situation? Which one and in what way?

3. Take a few minutes and write in paragraph form some of the patterns of struggle you may have in your marriage. Then, address these struggles by writing out how the tools apply. If you are doing this with your spouse, compare your paragraphs.

4. What specific Bible passages apply to your specific struggle? If you're not sure, ask a friend or use the concordance in the back of your Bible to locate a few. As a couple, commit them to memory.

5. Are there struggles you used to have that you have been able to resolve? How have you grown throughout your marriage? Take time to pray together and thank God for his grace and mercy.

Chapter 10

Forgiveness and Grace in Communication

People disqualify themselves from being forgiven
if they are so hardened in their own bitterness
that they cannot or will not forgive others.[1]

- D. A. Carson

So also my heavenly Father will do to every one of you,
if you do not forgive your brother from your heart.

- Matthew 18:35

DO YOU REMEMBER the story of how our marriage got started? The story was way back in the Introduction. We were in a bad way to say the least. Both of us were hopeless that God could change us and help. We didn't believe that we would have the ability to endure in marriage, let alone celebrate it. How do you recover from words and events that create such destruction? How do you run a race that has gone on ahead of you after you've stumbled so tragically out of the gate? And how do you now trust someone whose words have been so harsh and unloving?

I have one word for you: *forgiveness*. Forgiveness is the medicine that was needed in the spring of 1997 in the Flood home. Forgiveness is the remedy for the brokenness in our marriages. Forgiveness is the oil that makes relationships work. And the absence of forgiveness is the explanation as to why so many of us have become hopeless in our marriages.

"But you have no idea what he or she did to me!" You're absolutely right—I don't. But Jesus does. He knows your pain. He has wept with you through your heartache. He has walked with you in the loneliness of your thoughts. He has carried you when you didn't have the strength to walk. And he loves you far too much to leave you in the bitter poison of unforgiveness. The same Savior who draws near to your broken heart is the One who calls you to forgive as he has forgiven you. Why should you forgive? Because Jesus calls you to do it, and because Jesus forgave.

A Study in Forgiveness

Nearly all of Matthew 18 focuses on forgiveness. Jesus starts with the seriousness of sin. But he quickly transitions to the seriousness of forgiveness and stays there. The lesson is clear: we are to have such a heart for the sinner that we eagerly forgive sin. That's it, plain and simple. As Peter attempts to grasp the weight of what Jesus is saying, he asks a critical question in verse 21: "Then Peter came up and said to him, "Lord, how often will my brother sin against me, and I forgive him? As many as seven times?"

Peter gets the audacity of it, and he is trying to understand the boundaries of Jesus's teaching. *Surely,* he thinks, *this can't be the open-ended proposition that it sounds like. Let me just clarify when enough is enough.* Jesus's response to him is a kick in the shins of pride. Are you ready for it? Are you sure? Well, here is verse 22: "Jesus said to him, 'I do not say to you seven times, but seventy times seven.'"

Let me ask you

- Do you find yourself in Peter's place thinking, *Surely this is enough?*
- Have you forgiven in the past and yet been sinned against again?
- Are you currently wrestling with forgiveness, holding your spouse hostage to the consequences of his or her sin?

It is important to answer questions like these as we process Matthew 18 together. Survey yourself to figure out where you are in relation to these things. Read with the hope of applying to these things the grace of God and the enormous treasure we've received. To help Peter and those who respond like Peter, Jesus tells the story of the unmerciful servant.

The Story of Unforgiveness

It would be best if you took some time right now to read the story for yourself in Matthew 18:23–35. However, here is a brief summary.

A king decided to settle his debts. One servant in particular owed a massive debt too large to pay. He pleaded for mercy, and the king forgave the debt. Later, others saw this same man demand another servant pay a far lesser debt. Rather than extend the forgiveness he was given, he imprisoned his fellow servant until his debt was paid in full. When word got back to the king, the king was furious. He revoked his offer of forgiveness and treated the man as the man had treated his fellow servant. In verse 35, Jesus gives us the lesson we're supposed to take with us from this story. "So also my heavenly Father will do to every one of you, if you do not forgive your brother from your heart." Jesus is making the point that how we forgive others flows out of how we've been forgiven by God. We are supposed to forgive others because God has forgiven us.

Let me make an important disclaimer here. As we explore the area of forgiveness, I have in mind broad categories of sin that affect most or all of us. There are other sins that deserve special attention when discussing forgiveness. These include adultery or physical or sexual abuse. If these sins have been committed against you, I'm so sorry. I do not want you to process this material as though I'm being cavalier about forgiveness. I understand special attention is needed, and I don't want you feeling glossed over or lumped together with the broader categories I'm talking about. Contact the authorities if the situation calls for it. I also encourage you to reach out to your pastor or a good friend who can help you get specialized help. You will most certainly need help processing what is right, good, healthy, and appropriate within this material. Whether restoration is ever achieved—or is even appropriate—is not the main point. The point is how we view sins we commit and sins committed against us in light of our sin against God. And that applies to us all.

Just like the king and his servant, the truth of the matter is that God has forgiven us of far more than we will ever be asked to forgive others. This raises the stakes for the disciples and makes it clear the reason Jesus tells the story. The way Peter thinks about the boundaries of forgiving is flawed at its core. Plainly stated, the boundaries surrounding our forgiveness ought to be placed where God places his. Forgiven people are expected to be forgiving people in return. The degree of our willingness to forgive others reflects our awareness of how much we have been forgiven. This is why the New Testament repeats the point of the parable, "As the Lord has forgiven you, so you must also forgive" (Colossians 3:13; see also Luke 6:37).

When we understand our debt and receive the merciful offer of God's forgiveness, we are forgiven. The genuineness of that exchange is then seen in how we treat someone who has sinned, who owes us a debt.

Forgiveness in Marriage

We know that Jesus did not tell this story to a group of married couples at a conference or special marriage event. This is not instruction only intended for husbands or wives. This is his expectation for all who call on his name. This is the fruit the presence and activity of his Spirit should bear.

It is worth noting that we sometimes afford ourselves the freedom to leave our cloak of Christianity hanging on the rack by the front door of our homes. We can behave at home in ways we'd never consider behaving elsewhere. We are Christians to the world, but not to our spouses or our children. This ought not to be! Our faith ought to be most clearly manifest in our homes. If we extend grace to anyone made in God's image, we ought to extend a double portion to our spouse.

The story of the unmerciful servant didn't need to have a tragic ending, and neither does your marriage. The right and good choice is available to you. If you are currently living in unforgiveness, love beckons you to a better way. It says, "No, don't make that choice! Go *this* way!" And even if you have made *that* choice time and again, the good and right choice to forgive as you've been forgiven is still available to you today.

Our communication in marriage is going to be replete with stumbles and failures. With the many words we say to a person over a lifetime, there will be many that we regret saying and perhaps even more we wish we never heard. Here is the bottom line: if your marriage is going to be one that communicates and communicates well, you will need to become adept at forgiveness. So we must apply this passage rigorously to our marriages. This is not a difficult process to understand, but it is not easy to do. Allow me to capture the marital application in just a few, simple steps that follow the three scenes from the parable.

Keep yourself grateful

This is where the servant failed and where we must not. Before you knew Christ, your debt assured you a hopeless future where you would have been judged for your sin. You had no defense. But when you prayed and asked the Lord to forgive you, you were (either literally or figuratively) on your face before the King pleading for his mercy. Allow me to remind you of this glorious news: *he was merciful to you.* You are forgiven.

This should change everything about you. It should change the taste of food and the enjoyment of laughter. It should change how you see the created world around you and what you think of the people in your life. It should change the way you look at trials and disappointments. It should change your perspective on everything because *it changes everything.*

You don't need to wait another minute to be grateful. When Paul provided the Ephesian church instructions for walking with Christ, he included the following in his teaching:

> …giving thanks always and for everything to God the Father in the name of our Lord Jesus Christ… (Ephesians 5:20)

In that one clause he covers all things at all times—"always and for everything." Remind yourself of your "forgiven-ness" every morning before your feet hit the ground. It will change how you brush your teeth or enjoy the hot water on your back in the shower. Call to mind your forgiven-ness as you pull into your parking space at work and it will change how you look at your tasks, your appointments, your coworkers, and your boss.

Remind yourself of your forgiven-ness when you pull into your driveway or sit at your dinner table or respond to a text from your spouse. It will change how you see what frustrates you and the little things you wish were different. It will change how you listen to your spouse and whether you choose to take up small offenses or overlook them in grace and mercy. You are a forgiven person who should be so overflowing with gratitude that those around you see the hope that is within you. This is not just for the outside world—this is for your spouse.

One practical application of keeping yourself grateful is fostering deep gratitude for your spouse. God has provided your spouse as a gift to you. Finding fault with your spouse is the same as finding fault in a present you've been given. Imagine a friend opening a Christmas gift from you and finding all of the things wrong with it. That lands on you, the giver, as criticism and judgment of the gift you chose, doesn't it? Most of us would never think of doing that. Yet, when we criticize our spouse or find fault, that's just what we're doing. Gratitude for the work of God in your life includes gratitude for the differences between you and your spouse. As you grow in gratitude, you find it much more joyful to give forgiveness.

Keep your spouse's sin in perspective

Again, this is where the servant failed. The differing amounts of debt are so immense that the point can't be missed: one hundred days of debt versus two hundred thousand years of debt. Yet, the servant exacted the same punishment from his debtor as he would have owed to the King. That is colossal injustice, and we all see it. But what does this failure look like in marriage?

It looks like a settled bitterness that keeps a growing list of wrongs. It looks like being hopeless for change. It sees past weaknesses and sins in the moment and projects them endlessly into the future as though there is no God. It says awkwardly but boldly that God can forgive your sin but you will not forgive your spouse's sin. This kind of unforgiveness spreads like yeast throughout the dough of your marriage, impacting every cell and every fiber of your relationship. It impacts your conversations about money, parenting, sex, or even house cleaning. You find the flavor of your marriage determined by unforgiveness, and it is bitter for both of you.

But what if your spouse has sinned grievously against you in ways you believe you've never sinned against God? Perhaps on a human level their sin really is far greater than yours. In a case like that, you might be thinking, *But Rob, I do have my spouse's sin in perspective. It really is that big.*

I don't want to diminish the pain your husband's sin has caused you. I do not want to make light of the impact of your wife's sin against you. I do want this parable from your Savior to have its full effect in your life. I want you to be freed from the bonds of unforgiveness to thrive freely in the grace made available to you by your merciful King.

When you compare your spouse's sin against you to your sin against him or her, you may have it right; their sin may be bigger. But that is not what the parable does. The parable compares the debt owed to us against the debt we owed to the King. The difference is not in the actions taken, but in whom the actions are against.

You and your spouse are both sinners; you are both creatures. When you sin against one another, that doesn't change the nature of who you are. But God is neither a sinner nor a creature. One single sin of the smallest variety (think of eating forbidden fruit) is sufficient to create an insurmountable debt that permanently separates you from him. We are not comparing tit for tat here. We are comparing debt for debt, and the accounting is not in our favor. In this way, we keep our spouse's sin in perspective; it is compared to what is created between us and God when we sin against God.

Don't put boundaries on your forgiveness

I've always pictured Peter being wide-eyed. He seems to have had vigor for life, an enthusiasm in all he did. Even though that vigor got him in trouble many times, I like that about him. Imagine how wide-eyed he got when he understood Jesus's point: "No boundaries, Peter. None."

That doesn't mean we treat all sin the same in the practical sense. It doesn't mean we continue to allow our spouse to treat us with disregard and disrespect (more on that in a bit). It does mean that our forgiving posture toward that sin should never have an expiration date. It ought to never run out. The shape it takes may change, even drastically. But it ought always to remain. We ought always to remain forgiving people because we always remain forgiven people.

So what of the chronic offender? What of the repeat adulterer or even the violent abuser? We can't fully treat those questions here, but let me just speak to the issue of forgiveness. Should we forgive them again?

In the truest sense of the word, regarding holding them indebted to us, the only application this passage allows is the plain answer, yes. But what might that look like? It should take the shape of what would be most pleasing to God and most helpful to the chronic sinner. In Matthew 18, if the person continues to sin, the response is not to go to him privately forever. It escalates. Forgiveness can escalate in its restrictions or earthly consequences. While the posture of the one sinned against is the same, the action of that person can change.

Forgiveness is not enabling. It is not overlooking heinous sin. It does not mean you stay in a dangerous situation because you're trying to live like Jesus. It doesn't mean you don't contact the authorities. It means your posture, while doing all of those wise and right things, is set on releasing them from the debt they owe you. Why? Because you are a forgiven person.*

Conclusion

Consider the greatness of the forgiveness God gave to us. It is more than sufficient to cover our sins and restore us to God. It is given to us to be enjoyed. Yet, it is so much more. It is given to us to *give*. We give forgiveness to those in need of it. That invariably means someone who has sinned. "But Rob, what if we run out of the grace to give again?"

One of our family's favorite hymns is "He Giveth More Grace" by Annie Flint. The first two verses of that hymn provide poetic instruction for us:

He giveth more grace as our burdens grow greater,
He sendeth more strength as our labors increase,
To added afflictions he addeth his mercy,
To multiplied trials he multiplies peace.

When we have exhausted our store of endurance,
When our strength has failed ere the day is half-done,
When we reach the end of our hoarded resources
Our Father's full giving is only begun.[2]

---

* For those in abusive relationships, it is important to note that forgiveness does not necessarily mean reconciliation. In some cases, it is unwise for relationships to return to a former state. Wisdom and counsel are needed to walk through such things.

Brothers and sisters, if we could but introduce into our marriages a faint reflection of the forgiveness we've received, we would see fruit abound. We'd see the activity of God move. The weight of hopelessness would be exchanged for the weight of grace. The yoke of slavery would be exchanged for the yoke of Christ. And we might yet see the goodness of the Lord in our marriages. May God make it so.

Discussion/Reflection Questions

1. If you are born-again, what two or three characteristics described you before Christ? What two to three words describe how you feel about all you've been forgiven? Create two lists.

2. Are there particular sins your spouse has committed against you that you are struggling to forgive? What are they? Why do you believe that is? How might this message address your reasons?

3. There were three application points under "Forgiveness in Marriage." (Keep Yourself Grateful; Keep Your Spouse's Sin in Perspective; Don't Put Boundaries on Your Forgiveness). Which of those three does your marriage need most? Which do you believe your marriage does best?

4. Related to the previous question, in which ways can communication in marriage further be complicated if a spouse fails in one or all of those things?

5. As you reflect upon the grace of God given to us in abundance, what thoughts come to your mind? Are they marked by faith? Are they marked by unbelief? Share honestly.

Chapter 11

Compassion: Where Grace and Mercy Meet

*Forbearance or patience should be our response
to unintentional actions due to the faults or carelessness
of another. Forgiveness should be our response
to the intentional or provocative acts of another.*[1]
- Jerry Bridges

*And above all these put on love,
which binds everything together in perfect harmony.*
- Colossians 3:14

WE SPENT THE last chapter discussing the implication of being forgiven people. Having been released from such a massive debt, how could we withhold forgiveness for someone else's much smaller debt? How do we find strength and motivation to forgive someone even when we're right to be offended? We do so by looking first and foremost to the cross. The cross is where we are reminded of who we were, who we now are, and what we are called to be. Whether on the mission field or at kitchen table, followers of Jesus never outgrow the need to start with our eyes on the gospel and what Jesus has done for us.

Perhaps you are reading this with your spouse and you've been processing the content together. Perhaps you're reading this and will immediately hand it to your spouse when you're done. Or maybe you're reading this very confident your spouse has no interest in this—or maybe even in you. In the face of these many differences, there are some commonalities.

First, as you seek to apply what you've learned in this book, you will do so imperfectly. Your sinful motivations will creep through and corrupt your implementation of these communication tools. Your patience will run out, and you will strike back rather than forgive. Your weaknesses will be revealed as you feel strained by your efforts. This is true regardless of the way your spouse participates in this book or in your marriage.

Second, your spouse will sin while you're trying to master your communication. He or she will at times be snarky, salty, or sarcastic and, of course, you will too. You may not be extended the forgiveness you're due. His tongue will betray you. Her lips will cut you. You will be offended, and you will need to decide what to do and how to respond. This is true regardless of the way your spouse participates in this book or in your marriage.

To this day, even during the writing of this book, my lips have betrayed me. My tongue has been a weapon of my heart that has been used against my dear wife. And, lest you feel too much sympathy for her, her lips and tongue have been used similarly against me. We sin in many ways, and we need more than communication tools to get us through.

Paul, apostle and fellow sinner, comes to our rescue with counsel that changes everything. If we dare follow his counsel, even when it hurts, we all will see the power of the Spirit and the glory of Christ in our marriages. We find his counsel in Colossians 3.

Christ, the Image of God

Up to this point in Colossians, Paul has been talking almost exclusively about the person and work of Jesus Christ. As he does so, he dips into its implications on our lives. This passage in Colossians 3 is preceded by one of the most glorious Christological passages in all of Scripture: Colossians 1:15–20. It's worth taking up the space here just to be sure you see it with your own eyes. Read it. Then read it again.

> He is the image of the invisible God, the firstborn of all creation. For by him all things were created, in heaven and on earth, visible and invisible, whether thrones or dominions or rulers or authorities—all things were created through him and for him. And he is before all things, and in him all things hold together. And he is the head of the body, the church. He is the beginning, the firstborn from the dead, that in everything he might be preeminent. For in him all the fullness of God was pleased to dwell, and through him to reconcile to himself all things, whether on earth or in heaven, making peace by the blood of his cross.

This is the Savior of the world. If you've placed your faith in Jesus Christ, this is *your* Savior. And this is the one who died for us all. He is the reason we can extend the forgiveness we talked about in chapter 10. He is the one to whom we look before we do anything else. Notice where verse 20 ends: "…making peace by the blood of his cross." The glorious Son of God shed his blood so that you and I could have peace.

Paul immediately goes on in verses 21 and 22 to highlight that this blood reconciles to God those who were alienated from God. If we are going to be honest, that is you and me. This great Savior has reconciled us to God and given us what we require in order to live at peace with one another. After chapter 2 holds out for us the need to protect this work of God in our lives, Paul arrives at chapter 3. It is an entire chapter instructing us how to live a life worthy of a Savior like this.

Counsel for the Chosen

For our purposes, we are going to look particularly at verses 1–14 of chapter 3. After Paul calls us to keep our minds fixed firmly on Christ, he names things that have no place in a Christ-follower's life—anger, wrath, malice, slander, obscene talk, and lies. Though perhaps we once walked in them (or may yet be walking in them), they must go. He then goes one step further by telling us not only what we should "put off" but what we should "put on."

> Put on then, as God's chosen ones, holy and beloved, compassionate hearts, kindness, humility, meekness, and patience, bearing with one another and, if one has a complaint against another, forgiving each other; as the Lord has forgiven you, so you also must forgive. And above all these put on love, which binds everything together in perfect harmony.

You see where he starts again in verse 12? He starts with the work of Christ in our lives. He sets our eyes on the cross and its implications. We are God's chosen ones, holy and beloved. Just like in Matthew 18 in our last chapter, we are forgiven, we are accepted, we are adopted, and we are secure in Christ. Not only are malice, wrath, and slander poor reflections of Christ, but they are also actions and attitudes far beneath our station. We are God's, and he is ours. With that as our starting place, we cannot end up in anger, wrath, or malice. We cannot use our lips for slandering. Your lips were made for more than that, and Paul lays out just what those things are.

He calls us to compassion. He calls us to forbearance. He calls us to kindness and patience and meekness. Do you know how easy it is to be compassionate if you're never near anyone who is sinning? Do you know how easy it is to be kind if you never have to relate to others? Anyone can do these things in isolation, but when we are in relationships of any kind, we are with sinners. We are with people who will push our buttons and treat us in ways they ought not. Every time we relate to someone—anyone—we have opportunity to exercise these things because people are imperfect. And this finds its full expression in marriage.

Your spouse has weaknesses. Your spouse has besetting sins. Those weaknesses and sins are going to overflow onto and into your life. You will respond; that much is certain. The question is how? Will you respond as someone who has never been reconciled to God, or will you respond as one who is chosen and dearly loved by God? Will we love as the rest of the world loves, or will we choose to love as Christ loves?

Anatomy of Mercy

Jesus was asked for many things when he walked on this earth. One of the most frequent requests was for mercy: "Son of David, have mercy on us." Mercy is desired by all as a gift to receive, but it is less desirable when we are called to give it. The principle is clear: it is much easier to receive mercy than it is to give it. Yet, give it we must. The master in the Matthew 18 parable asks the rhetorical question of the unmerciful servant, "And should not you have had mercy on your fellow servant, as I had mercy on you?" (verse 33).

Mercy can be elusive because mercy is complex. It requires some ingredients that float just below the surface and, if we're not perceptive or careful, we'll miss them and miss mercy in the process. You see, in order for mercy to exist, there first must be an offender.

The offender

The offender is the one who sins against someone. He or she is bringing the offense. Some situations are clear and grievous examples of sin. Perhaps there has been lying or cheating or adultery or addictions that have led to brokenness in your marriage. Perhaps there has been anger or neglect that has left you wondering how and why. These are just some of the ways husbands and wives may fill the role of offender.

Yet it's not always that clear cut, particularly in marriage. Too often we look to our spouses to be more than they're supposed to be. We want our spouses to be sinless so that they are always a blessing to us. We want our spouses to be mind readers so that they can always be intuitive and care for us. We want our spouses to be free from weakness so that anything that might bring a stumbling block to us would be eliminated. Essentially, we want our spouses to function like little "christs," when we should be looking to the Living Christ for those things. When our spouse sins or lives out of a weakness in their lives, he or she brings the offense. But that's just the first ingredient. If we have an "offender," we need to have an "offended."

The offended

For our purposes, that is you. That is you when your spouse forgets to do what you've asked or fails to inquire about your hard day. This is you when your spouse struggles yet again with a besetting sin or a chronic area of weakness. That is you when your spouse sins grievously and devastates you, your marriage, and your family. They offend, and you receive the offense. In some cases, this is necessary because the sin is serious. In other cases, we need to get better at letting offenses go. But in either case, we have the first two necessary ingredients for mercy: an offender and an offended. You cannot have mercy if there is no object to receive it. You cannot have mercy if there is no person positioned to give it.

Here's where we stand:

Offender + Offended + _____ = Mercy

Pay special attention here, because this is the point where things turn toward good or bad, toward righteousness or wickedness, toward unity or division. YOU bring the final ingredient, and what you bring will determine whether you arrive at the mercy to which you're called.

Let's say you, the offended, bring the final ingredient of anger. You know you've been sinned against, and you've had it. You respond out of that anger. Look at how the equation works then:

Offender + Offended + Anger = Revenge

That sounds quite a lot like the ingredients we've been told to "put off": anger, wrath, and malice. This is the very thing that Romans 12:19 tells us to leave to God. There are marriages that are marked with constant fighting, nasty communication, and unending division. There is a genuine offender and one who is genuinely offended. However, they themselves add "anger" and both suffer for it. It's tragic for so many reasons. First, it's a very hard way to live. Second, it is such a poor reflection of the image of Christ and his church.

Sometimes, the offended brings the final ingredient of self-pity rather than anger. That changes the equation entirely:

Offender + Offended + Self-Pity = Victim

Now, there are abuse situations where someone truly is a victim. That is not in view here. What is in view is a person who has received ordinary offense and responds with disproportionate self-pity. When you feel sorry for yourself, it is a challenge to feel compassion for someone else.

The fundamental problem with both of these approaches (anger and self-pity) is that they reflect a self-focus rather than a Christ-focus. Rather than looking to the cross, we're looking in a mirror. We ought to be saying, "Because I've received so much mercy, I must give it." But rather, we say, "I don't deserve to be treated like that, and I'm getting even" or "I deserve to be treated like that so I'm just going to take it." WE are in view, rather than Christ. If we change our starting point by looking first to Christ, look what happens to the equation:

Offender + Offended + Compassion = Mercy

As God's chosen and dearly loved, verse 12 calls us to compassionate hearts. This means you see each offense and each weakness as an opportunity for compassion. You understand that you're married to an imperfect, incomplete person, and you are resolved that it's okay. You will love regardless, maybe even more so. You will be patient with the slow growth of your spouse, extending understanding and compassion. You will bear with your spouse in areas where you wish he or she was different.

With compassion on the scene, mercy becomes possible. You love your spouse as he or she is, and you don't withhold your love until he or she changes to be as you wish. You show compassion and bend toward them, being willing to cross the midline for the sake of love, for the sake of mercy, for the sake of the glory of Christ. Sound impossible? Remember, this is how God loves us. And he empowers us to love others as he has loved us. In Christ, it is possible.

Where Grace and Forgiveness Meet

Richard Sibbes, in his book *The Bruised Reed*, wrote,

> It would be a good contest amongst Christians, one to labour to give no offence, and the other to labour to take none. The best men are severe to themselves, tender over others.[2]

Can you imagine it? A home where there is an ongoing contest to see who can give the least offense and who can take up the least offense? Imagine the impact on a marriage if each spouse took up this challenge to "outdo one another in showing honor" (Romans 12:10). How is this even possible?

It is the natural outflow of a life lived for Christ. It is the overflow of a heart that has received more grace and forgiveness than can be measured. It is the instinct of a life that is changed for eternity. It is the reflex of humility that realizes the offenses we receive are nothing compared to the wrath that was due us. It is the outcome of a life lived at the foot of Calvary.

When you live with a posture of forgiveness toward your spouse, you are willing to extend grace. And when grace and forgiveness are allowed to coexist, to live side by side and become the best of friends, you develop the compassionate heart that ought to exist in the chests of all who are God's chosen, holy and dearly loved.

Marriage with the Cross in View

In her book *How to Act Right When Your Spouse Acts Wrong*, Leslie Vernick diagnoses our underlying problem.

> We need to begin living at the point where everything, and nothing short of that, is about the glory of God. That is the end for which we were made and, as Christians, that is the end for which we should live. Yet many of us have made an exchange. We have devalued living for God's glory and have valued living for something else as our ultimate satisfaction in life. For many of us, the shift has been subtle but the erosion steady.[3]

Unsurprisingly, this is precisely where Paul takes us at the end of this passage in Colossians 3:17:

> And whatever you do, in word or deed, do everything in the name of the Lord Jesus, giving thanks to God the Father through him.

You are married to an image bearer of the living God. If your spouse is a believer, you are also married to one of God's chosen, elect, and adopted saints. Paul has called us to do "everything in the name of the Lord Jesus." Your marriage is included in "everything," and you are called to give thanks to God the Father for it.

Thank you is good to say and much better to live out. If you are going to be a husband or wife to the glory of God, it will require that you do so with the love that God supplies. You will need to employ the mercy you've been given. You will need to depend upon the Spirit as your helper. You will need to extend forgiveness since you've received it in abundance. And you will need to make Christ your goal, not fixing or judging or adjusting your spouse.

If God's people would live out their marriages in this way, we would all see the unity and love and trust and care that God desires. We'd put marriage counselors out of business and marriages within the church would stand head and shoulders above those in our culture. The watching world would look on and wonder at why these homes, these marriages are so different. And we'd have integrity along with increased opportunity to tell the world of our gracious, patient, forgiving, merciful, and loving Savior.

Discussion/Reflection Questions

1. What are some of the areas of your marriage you wish would see significant improvement? List them here in priority order.

2. Consider two to three areas of preference you wish were different in your spouse. (Not areas of overt sin, but of preference.) What would happen if you overlooked them and never spoke to them? What if you accepted them as a part of who your spouse is?

3. What ingredient are *you* most often bringing to being offended that distracts from mercy?

4. Envision what your marriage would look like if you applied this message. What would be different? What change could occur tonight or tomorrow if applied? Write your thoughts here.

5. How can giving thanks change your perspective on the disappointing areas of your marriage? How can it buoy hope and help you move forward as a couple?

The Communication Vow

AT THE BEGINNING of the book, I encouraged you to pray for some very specific things. I asked that you pray that God would reveal your own weaknesses and sins in communication, rather than you focusing on the faults of your spouse. And I asked you to pray that God would bring more than clarity, but also conviction, insight, and hope. I sincerely hope that God has answered those prayers and done just that. What's next?

Communication is not an elective course in marriage; it is core material. Regardless of age, financial status, length of marriage, number of children, or geographic location, all couples must communicate. Facing that reality, we apply ourselves to move ever more closely to healthy patterns of communication.

On your wedding day you spoke wedding vows of some sort. You made promises to your spouse before clergy, before family and friends, and before God himself. The traditional wedding vows typically go something like this: I take you to be my wedded wife/husband, to have and to hold from this day forward, for better, for worse, for richer, for poorer, in sickness and in health, to love and to cherish, till death do us part.

Maybe you wrote your own vows. This can be sweet and romantic. It gives you an opportunity to bring a personal touch to your wedding. But sometimes self-authored wedding vows are actually no vows at all. They sometimes are void of any promise for commitment or conduct and simply express love and affection.

When I perform weddings, in addition to the vows couples may write themselves, I always include the traditional vows somewhere in the ceremony. They contain actual promises in areas where I'm confident each couple will be tested. Revisiting these vows can be a healthy habit to remind ourselves what we promised to do. You may find there is some dusting off to do or sharpening to pursue.

As with marriage vows, it can be helpful to have resolutions and vows in other areas of life. Jonathan Edwards was famous for his many resolutions on how he was going to live his life. Allow me to offer a Communication Vow for you to read and consider claiming for yourself. You need not read this out loud in a ceremony, though you may consider doing so with your spouse in private. A vow like this can be helpful to keep handy on a refrigerator or on a bathroom mirror as a regular reminder of what you've committed to in your marital communication.

With These Words
A Communication Vow

With these words
   I will seek to build you up rather than tear you down.
With these words
   I will do all I can to reiterate what you mean in a way that honors and respects you.

With these hands
>> I will touch you caringly, seeking unity even
>> through the hardest conversations.

With these eyes
>> I will look on you tenderly, avoiding judgment
>> and scorn.

With these ears
>> I will listen intently to understand what you're
>> trying to say.

With this heart
>> I will seek to love the Lord first and foremost,
>> loving you all the while.

With these words
>> I will share grace, mercy, and forgiveness as it has
>> abundantly been shared with me by our Savior.

And with God's help
>> our communication will draw us more closely
>> together
>>> for the good of our home and the glory of
>>> God.

A Closing Prayer

As we started the book praying together, it is my desire to conclude in the same manner. We've covered a lot of ground. As you close this book and seek to apply it, consider starting with one tool at a time. Trust God through the process. Depend on God's grace. Give your spouse even more grace. And expect God to move. He delights in obedience, and he is pleased to act on behalf of marriage.

Father, you've been kind to provide for us instruction and encouragement toward doing your will. You've entrusted to us the powerful instrument of words. Please give us your Spirit to guide us in all truth so that we would use that power for good and not for evil, so that we would love as we are loved, forgive as we've been forgiven, and extend mercy even as it has been extended to us. Help my spouse to know you better and love you more, and use me as you see fit to bring about those ends. Take my marriage, Lord, and use it for your glory. Help me be more like Christ in my role, and may you be pleased to help our communication grow.

"Now to him who is able to keep you from stumbling and to present you blameless before the presence of his glory with great joy, to the only God, our Savior, through Jesus Christ our Lord, be glory, majesty, dominion, and authority, before all time and now and forever. Amen" (Jude 24–25).

Endnotes

Chapter 1

1. Gary Edward Schnittjer, *The Torah Story: An Apprenticeship on the Pentateuch* (Grand Rapids: Zondervan, 2010), Chapter 5.

Chapter 2

1. Thomas Watson, *A Godly Man's Picture* (Edinburgh: Banner of Truth, 2009), 179.

Chapter 3

1. John Piper, "The Mouth of the Righteous Is a Fountain of Life," (Desiring God, sermon, 1991), https://www.desiringgod.org/messages/the-mouth-of-the-righteous-is-a-fountain-of-life.
2. Piper, "The Mouth of the Righteous.

Chapter 4

1. J. K. Rowling, *Harry Potter and the Chamber of Secrets*, Book 2, Harry Potter (New York: Scholastic, 2000), 333.
2. Gina Flood, "Gentleness" (Covenant Fellowship Church, 2010), expired blog.

Chapter 5

1. R. A. Torrey, *Your Life in God* (New Kensington: Whitaker House, 2002), ebook.

2. Among the many books on prayer that I'd recommend, the following five provide a great starting point: *The Power of Prayer in a Believer's Life* by Charles Spurgeon; *Valley of Vision* by Arthur Bennett; *A Praying Life* by Paul Miller; *It Happens After Prayer* by H. B. Charles, Jr.; and *Two Hearts Praying As One* by Dennis and Barbara Rainey.

3. Torrey, *Your Life in God.*

Chapter 6

1. John Keats, To — (What can I do to drive away), undated, public domain.

Chapter 9

1. Richard Foster, *Celebration of Discipline: The Path to Spiritual Growth*, Special Anniversary Edition (New York: HarperOne, 2018), 107.

2. Although based upon my own insights and experience with couples in counseling, these couples are fictional and there is no intention to reflect anyone specific, either in name or situation.

Chapter 10

1. D. A. Carson, *Love in Hard Places* (Wheaton: Crossway, 2002), 79.

2. Annie J. Flint, "He Giveth More Grace," public domain.

Chapter 11

1. Jerry Bridges, *Transforming Grace* (Colorado Springs: Navpress, 1991), 204.

2. Richard Sibbes, *The Bruised Reed* (Edinburgh: Banner of Truth, 2005), 23.

3. Leslie Vernick, *How to Act Right When Your Spouse Acts Wrong* (Colorado Springs: Waterbrook Press, 2001), 100.